MEMORIALS

OF THE

EARLY LIVES AND DOINGS

OF

GREAT LAWYERS.

By

C. L. BRIGHTWELL,

Author of "The Life of Mrs. Opie," "Annals of Industry and Genius,"
&c. &c.

THE LAWBOOK EXCHANGE, LTD.
Union, New Jersey
2002

ISBN 1-58477-236-0

Second reprinting 2004

Printed in the United States of America
on acid-free paper

The Lawbook Exchange, Ltd.
33 Terminal Avenue
Clark, New Jersey 07066-1321

Please see our website for a selection of our other publications
and fine facsimile reprints of classic works of legal history:
www.lawbookexchange.com

Library of Congress Cataloging-in-Publication Data

Brightwell, C. L. (Cecilia Lucy), 1811-1875.
Memorials of the early lives and doings of great lawyers / by C.L. Brightwell.
p. cm.
Originally published: London: T. Nelson and Sons, 1866.
ISBN 1-58477-236-0 (cloth: alk. paper)
1. Lawyers—Great Britain—Biography. 2. Practice of law—Great Britain—History. I. Title.

KD536 .B75 2002
340'.092'241—dc21
[B] 2002025959

MEMORIALS

OF THE

EARLY LIVES AND DOINGS

OF

GREAT LAWYERS.

By

C. L. BRIGHTWELL,

Author of "The Life of Mrs. Opie," "Annals of Industry and Genius,"
&c. &c.

LONDON
T. NELSON AND SONS, PATERNOSTER ROW;
EDINBURGH; AND NEW YORK.

1866.

This Little Book

IS AFFECTIONATELY DEDICATED

TO

HER NEPHEWS,

TOM AND HARRY BRIGHTWELL,

BY

THEIR LOVING AUNT,

CECILIA LUCY BRIGHTWELL.

PREFACE

IN this little volume will be found a series of short biographical notices of some of our most renowned English lawyers, having reference principally to the earlier period of their lives, and occasionally detailing a few of their more remarkable "sayings and doings."

From Lord Campbell's "Lives of the Chief-Justices" and of "the Chancellors" I have principally derived my information; and to those delightful volumes the young student is directed, that he may acquaint himself with these illustrious characters in full-drawn portraiture.

This work, designed as a school-prize book, will, it is hoped, stir the mind of many a youth to emulate the worthy example and tread in the footsteps of the eminent men who have from age to age filled the highest places in our Courts of Judicature, and who are among the greatest benefactors and brightest ornaments of our nation.

CONTENTS

LIVES AND DOINGS

OF

GREAT LAWYERS.

Introduction.

WHILE engaged in preparing these biographical sketches for the press, I have frequently called to remembrance an evening I spent, many years ago, in company with the eminent and well-known jurist, the late Mr. John Austin. I saw him under very favourable circumstances, when none were present but his intimate friends and connections, and he was drawn into a long and deeply interesting talk. On returning home I took notes of what he had said, and as some of his observations had reference to the subject of jurisprudence, I have determined to give them here.

After he had been speaking at some length on the subject of languages and dialects, the conversation took a different turn. My father was desirous to obtain Mr. Austin's opinion respecting the question of law as relating to the Christian economy—to the religion of the

New Testament. On this point he stated it to be his opinion that the sanctions of the gospel are drawn from a higher source—that, in fact, there is no such thing as statute or law laid down in the New Testament. The appeal is made to another and higher principle, superior to all the sanctions of law, and having its source from within;—in which sense he understood the passage in the Romans, "Being a law to themselves," as he said this was a metaphorical expression, and could not be literally taken; it being impossible for a man to make laws for himself, the fact being evident that he could at any time abrogate a self-imposed rule. He further went on to observe, respecting the much contested subject of the freedom of the will, that, in his opinion, there could be no such thing, for that it resolved itself into a question of choice or object—the bondage of the will to sin and evil being exchanged for a *subjection* of the will to higher influences.

He said, in reference to Christianity, that it is decidedly the most *original* thing that has ever been presented to view in our world; that its character is entirely unique; and that any man deeply acquainted with history, and able to go back along the records it gives, must feel that the influence of Christianity has done more to *humanize* than any other cause. Anybody looking into the laws of the more excellent among the emperors—of the Antonines and Adrians, and those called models of piety and goodness—will be at once convinced of the truth of this. The slave is put beyond the pale of humanity; the influence of the principle, "Do to others as you would that they should do to you," is unknown, unfelt; nor is such a sanction anywhere to be found, taken in its true extent, but in the Christian religion. "Christianity," said he, "is *humanizing;* and in this, its distinguishing characteristic, is found its infinite superiority. . . ."

This is a striking testimony to the peculiar, the blessed "*humanizing*" influence of Christianity; an influence which of necessity affects both the formation and the execution of the laws wherever it has sway, although, alas! so partially has its leaven been permitted to operate, that, even in our happy land, the life and liberty of men have not been secure from outrage under legal sanction. Within the last half century, in the heart of the venerable city I inhabit, a terrible tragedy was enacted. Two fine young men, farmers' servants, were hanged on the top of the Castle Hill, in the sight of hundreds of their fellows, for the sole crime of having stolen a lamb!

The assembled multitude gazed with feelings of aversion and terror, for it was felt to be nothing short of a legal murder. *Vox populi*—that irresistible voice, when uttered in the cause of humanity and right—pronounced it such. Since that fatal day there has been no such horror enacted; it was the last example of the kind.

We owe hearty thanks to those noble-minded advocates who have lifted up their cry in remonstrance against the harsh and bloody laws which but recently disgraced our statute books. Among those illustrious names, that of Sir Samuel Romilly ranks high. Undoubtedly there is no profession in this country which exerts so important an influence upon our social and political relations as that of the Law, and it has accordingly been always a road to the highest stations in the land. Upon the whole, the history of our nation tells much in favour of those who have distinguished themselves at the bar and on the bench, many of whom, in the worst and darkest times, have nobly vindicated the rights of the people and the prerogatives of the crown. In how many instances have the liberties of England been preserved by the intrepidity and independence of the judges of the land! Thus, for example, in alluding to the unconstitutional attempts of the Stuarts to subvert our privileges, Mr. Godwin says, "It is impossible to review these proceedings without feeling that for these liberties we are to no man so deeply indebted as to Sir Edward Coke." That great man, so learned a lawyer and eminent a judge, was also a devoted patriot, zealously attached to the law, satisfied that it afforded the best guarantee for the liberties of the subject and the rights of the crown.

Accordingly, it was well observed of him that "he lost his advantage in the same way he got it—by his tongue." "And," adds the quaint historian, "long lived he in the retirement to which court indignation had remitted him; yet was not his recess inglorious, for, at improving a disgrace to the best advantage, he was so excellent as King James said of him, 'He was like a cat, throw him which way you will he will light upon his feet!'"

It is unhappily true that all our judges have not walked in the steps of this illustrious personage, and history has registered the misdeeds and unblushing corruption of but too many of their number. Lord Bacon, in his history of the reign of Henry VII., writes in words of burning indignation concerning those rapacious judges who enriched themselves and the king by their exactions and preying, as he says, "like tame hawks for their master, and like wild hawks for themselves." It is a melancholy reflection that this great genius, who in his writings and in his exhortations to the judges denounces the sinfulness of accepting bribes, was, by his own confession, repeatedly guilty of the same crime. Indeed, that melancholy period in which the Stuart dynasty bore rule abounds with instances of judicial corruption, though relieved by occasional bright exceptions. In the famous case of "Ship Money," the judges were almost unanimous for the king. One of their number, Mr. Justice Croke, although convinced that the law was opposed to the claims of the crown, finding the voices of his brethren against him, and fearing lest his resistance should prove unavailing, and merely result in his own loss of place and the consequent ruin of his family, had at length determined to yield and to concur with the other judges in a decision favourable to the court. A few days before he had to argue, we are told by the historian Whitelock, "upon discourse with some of his nearest relations and most serious thoughts of the business," he intimated his intention, when his wife, who was a very good and pious woman, told him that "she hoped he would do nothing against his conscience for fear of any danger or prejudice to her or his family, and that she would be contented to suffer want or any misery with him rather than be an occasion for him to do or say anything against his judgment and conscience."

The heroic counsel of this admirable woman prevailed, and when the hour of danger came her husband was firm in his allegiance to the cause of truth and of his country.

In the present day the integrity of our judges is not put to such severe trial, and we are in no danger of judicial corruption. Such stumbling-blocks as these do not lie in the path of the aspirant to legal distinction now. To rise in the profession of the law, a man must bear an unblemished character and repute. But, in this, as in other roads to wealth and honour, "iter per ardua ad astra." They who are most competent to speak on such matters affirm that the study and practice of the law are far from an easy task. Legal training is laborious, and in some branches dry and unattractive, and one must work hard in order to become conversant with

> "The gathered wisdom of a thousand years."

It is only by diligence and persevering, energetic effort that the prize can be won and the difficulties of the ascent surmounted. A laborious profession it must ever be, but what a worthy and honourable one—to be pursued with an approving conscience, and without the terrible penalties associated with military ambition.

I.

Sir Thomas More.

Cromwell. Sir Thomas More is chosen
Lord Chancellor, in your place.
Wolsey. That's somewhat sudden:
But he's a learned man. May he continue
Long in his Highness' favour, and do justice
For truth's sake, and his conscience; that his bones,
When he has run his course, and sleeps in blessings,
May have a tomb of orphans' tears wept on 'em.
Henry VIII., Act iii., Scene 2.

THE event thus chronicled by our great dramatist took place on the 25th October, 1529, when, in a council held at Greenwich, King Henry VIII. delivered the Great Seal to Sir Thomas More, and constituted him Lord Chancellor of England.

This admirable man, so interesting in his life and in his death, was, at the time of his elevation, in the forty-ninth year of his age, and had acquired a great fame, not only among his own countrymen, but with the great and good of various nations, for his wisdom, integrity, and goodness. One cannot imagine a more lovely and attractive picture than that which is presented of him by his contemporaries; and we love him in his household character fully as much as we admire and reverence his learning. He was born in 1480, and was a son of Sir

Thomas More, a judge of the Court of King's Bench, who was of a respectable family, and entitled by his descent to use an armorial bearing, a privilege guarded strictly and jealously by those who then began to be called gentry.

The lawyers in those days lived in the city, and young More first saw the light in Milk Street, Cheapside, then a fashionable quarter of the metropolis. Until his fifteenth year he was put to St. Anthony's School, in Threadneedle Street, a seminary in high repute, and which produced Archbishops Heath and Whitgift, as well as many other eminent men.

It was the custom of that age that young gentlemen should pass part of their boyhood in the house and service of their superiors in rank, that they might profit by observing the manners and listening to the conversation of their patrons, and gradually acquire a similitude to those whom they could only in this way have an opportunity of approaching. It was not considered derogatory to young men of good breeding that they should be trained, during this noviciate, to render humble and even menial offices; and a young gentleman was willing and anxious to offer his services as the page of a great man, that he might enjoy advantages otherwise unattainable. However strange this may seem to us, it is perhaps not more so than the custom of *fagging* in our public schools, to which boys in a good rank of life are even now obliged to submit. In accordance with this usage, when he had reached the age of fifteen, Thomas More became a page in the family of Cardinal Morton, Archbishop of Canterbury, one of Henry VII.'s most able ministers. His services and long experience in affairs had procured him the highest offices, and he continued prime minister until his death, which happened in the year 1500, when he had attained the patriarchal age of ninety. At the time when More entered his household, the cardinal, though more than fourscore years old, was pleased with the extraordinary promise of the sharp and lively boy, and had the sagacity to discern his extraordinary merit, and to foretell the future celebrity of his page. In the rude dramas performed on occasion of the Christmas festivities in the cardinal's palace, the lad distinguished himself, taking a forward part—probably as competitor in those contests of extempore wit and drollery which were the delight of the age. Pleased with the readiness and obliging manners of his ward, the old man would point to him and say, "The child here waiting at table will some day prove a marvellous rare man." On his part, the youth fully appreciated the excellencies of his patron, and thus described him:—"In his face did shine such an amiable reverence as was pleasant to behold. In speech he was fine, eloquent, and pithy. In the law he had profound knowledge. In wit he was incomparable, and in memory excellent. These qualities, which were in him by nature, he by learning and use had made perfect." Probably it was while in the cardinal's household that More was first known to Collet, Dean of St. Paul's, and future founder of St. Paul's School, who used to say there was but one wit in England, and that one was young Thomas More.

By the advice of his patron, who took great care of his bringing up, the lad was sent, at the age of seventeen, to Oxford, where he lodged at New Hall, but studied at Canterbury College—afterwards Christ Church. He must have lived a very different life there to that he had enjoyed in the archiepiscopal palace, for "in his allowance his father kept him very short, scarcely suffering him to have so much money in his hands as would pay for the mending of his apparel, and expecting from him a particular account of his expenses,"—a parsimony for which his son, though dissatisfied at the time, afterwards thanked him, affirming that he was thereby curbed from all vice, and withdrawn from gaming and naughty company.

He remained thus above two years, studying very diligently, and cultivating with great enthusiasm the knowledge of the Greek literature, recently introduced in the university by certain learned scholars who had acquired it in Italy;—Grocyn, the first professor of Greek in the university; Linacre, the accomplished founder of the College of Physicians; and Collet, who had spent four years abroad in the same studies.

There was great excitement prevailing among the students, and a sort of civil war waged between the partisans of the Greek learning, who were the innovators in education, and suspected of heresy, and perhaps infidelity, on the one hand, and on the other side the older, more powerful and celebrated men, who were content to tread in the old paths; especially the Established clergy, who, although not yet alarmed by Luther's attacks, were inimical to the new studies, and could not endure the prospect of a rising generation more learned than themselves.

Our young and ardent student entered with zeal into the contest, and expostulated with the university in a letter addressed to the whole body, reproaching them with the better example of Cambridge, where the gates were thrown open to the higher classics of Greece as freely as to their Roman imitators.

At Oxford More became acquainted with the illustrious scholar Erasmus, who was then reading at the university, having been invited to England by Lord Mountjoy, when his pupil at Paris. Resembling each other in their genius, their tastes, and their acute observation of character and manners, their lively sense of the ridiculous, their constant hilarity, and their devotion to classical lore, they soon formed a close friendship, notwithstanding the great disparity in their years, Erasmus being then thirty, and More only seventeen. This mutual attachment lasted through life, without interruption or abatement; and was fostered during absence by an epistolatory correspondence, still preserved, and affording the most striking sketches of the history and customs of the times in which they lived.

We are told that, while at the university More "profited exceedingly in rhetoric, logic, and philosophy," and likewise distinguished himself much by the composition of poems, both in Latin and English, which are interesting as proofs of his extraordinary precocity, and as the exercises by which he acquired facility in the arts of oratory and composition.

Having completed his course at Oxford, he forthwith applied himself to the study of the law, which was to be the occupation of his life. He first studied at New Inn, and afterwards at Lincoln's Inn.* There were taught the more profound and abstruse branches of the science

* The term *inn* was successively applied, like the French word *hotel*, first to the town mansion of a great man, and afterwards to a house of general entertainment for money; and the societies of lawyers having purchased some inns or noblemen's residences in London, these were hence called Inns of Court.

by learned professors, and efficient tests of proficiency were applied before the degree of barrister was conferred, entitling the aspirant to practise as an advocate.

In a short time More was appointed reader at Furnival's Inn, where he delivered lectures for three years with great applause. "After this," says his son-in-law, "to his great commendation he read for a good space a public lecture of St. Augustine, *De Civitate Dei*, in the church of St. Lawrence, in the Old Jewry; whereunto there resorted Doctor Grocyn, an excellent cunning man, and all the chief learned of the city of London."

This seems to us a strange business, that a young lawyer should read divinity lectures on the moral government of the world. But it must be remembered that the clergy were then the chief depositaries of knowledge, as they had been for a long time the only lawyers; and religion, morals, and law, were taught without due distinction. It appears, moreover, from the report of his loving relative, More did not so much discuss the points of divinity, as the precepts of moral philosophy and history contained in those books.

Strange as it may seem, in the midst of this excitement and popularity the young lecturer was seized with a desire to renounce the world and its busy ways, and to embrace the monastic life. Attracted by the holy pleasures of piety, or touched with the idea of superior sanctity, and enamoured of the glory of St. Augustine, he resolved to enter the order of St. Francis, and for this purpose took a lodging close by the great Carthusian monastery, called the Charter House, and began as a lay brother to practise severe austerities, preparatory to taking the irrevocable vows. For some time he added penance to penance, mortifying himself by watching and fasting, seldom allowing himself more than four or five hours' sleep, and lying on the floor or on a hard bench. In addition to all this, he had recourse to self-flagellations; and it is pitiable to know that, to a certain extent, this good and great man remained through life the slave of such superstitions, retaining to the last his hair shirt and his knotted cord. To account for such things we must remember the instructions and habits of his education, and bear in mind that he was ever conscientiously devoted to the Church of which he was a member.

Happily he soon became convinced by these proceedings that nature had not fitted him to play the part of a hermit; and he presently relinquished the idea of taking orders, determined to marry, and having returned to his profession, exerted all his energies in its pursuit, that he might rise to distinction, and be able creditably to maintain his family. "God had allotted him for another state—not to live solitary, but that he might be a pattern to reverend married men how they should carefully bring up their children, how dearly they should love their wives, how they should employ their endeavours wholly for the good of their country, yet excellently perform the virtues of religious men, as piety, humility, obedience, yea, conjugal chastity."

There must indeed have been something singularly sweet and loving in his nature, very winning to his associates, and deeply felt by them, insomuch that Erasmus scarcely ever concludes a letter to him without epithets indicating the most tender affection rather than the calm relationship of friendship; thus he designates him repeatedly "*suavissime*," "*charissime*," and "*melli-*

tissime More." Such a nature was singularly well adapted to domestic life, and none more exquisitely enjoyed its blessings.

His descendant gives a curious account of the young lawyer's courtship. It seems he made the acquaintance of an Essex gentleman, a Mr. J. Colt, of New Hall, who invited him to his house, and introduced him to his three daughters, pleasant country girls, young and well-looking. The second was the most agreeable to his fancy; he thought her the prettiest, but as the elder one would have felt herself slighted by being passed over in favour of her younger sister, he decided to pay his addresses to her, and in a short time they were married, "to the good liking of all her friends." One of his biographers says: "He settled her in a house in Bucklersbury, where they lived in uninterrupted harmony and affection. There never was a happier union. He now applied himself, with unremitted assiduity, to the business of his profession, being stimulated and cheered and comforted and rewarded by her smiles. He soon rose very rapidly at the bar, and was particularly famous for his skill in international law."

About the same time we find him appointed to the office of under-sheriff of London, an office then judicial, and of considerable dignity. In this capacity his duties seem to have been very onerous and extensive. Erasmus says that his Court was held every Thursday, and that no judge of that Court ever went through more causes; none decided them more uprightly;—often remitting the fees to which he was entitled from the suitors. His deportment in this capacity endeared him extremely to his fellow-citizens.

A crisis in the history of More was at hand. He had reached his twenty-fourth year, when he was returned to the House of Commons, "many having now taken notice of his sufficiency;" and he is honourably recorded in the history of our country as being the first person who gained celebrity as a speaker in the House; and who, as a successful leader of opposition, incurred the enmity of the Court. The King demanded an extravagant subsidy on occasion of his daughter's marriage with James IV. of Scotland; and the consent of the Lower House was about to be given, most of the members, however unwilling to submit to these impositions, fearing to oppose the royal will. But our young member arose, and in a grave and impressive speech, urged such reasons why these exactions should not be granted, that the general spirit was roused, and the subsidy refused. "Upon this, Mr. Tyler, one of the King's Privy Chamber, went presently from the House, and told his Majesty that a beardless boy had disappointed him of all his expectations."

Great was the indignation of the King, and he vowed to have his revenge; but, as the youthful offender had nothing himself to lose, Henry had recourse to the mean expedient of raising a causeless quarrel against More's father, confining him in the Tower till he had made him pay a heavy fine. Nor did the royal spite end here. The young patriot was regarded with an evil eye, and an opportunity carefully watched to bring about his ruin. In consequence, he determined to quit his native land, feeling that there was no security for him in England. Meanwhile, he prudently had recourse to the expedient of concealing himself from remark by withdrawing almost entirely from his practice at the bar, and living in retirement, while he devoted himself assiduously to the cultivation of his mind, "perfecting himself in most of the liberal sciences, as music, arithmetic, geometry, and astronomy, and growing to be a perfect historian." He also studied the French language, and "sometimes recreated his tired spirits on the viol."

In such pursuits he passed some four or five years, when the death of Henry VII. released him from his fears, and called him again into public life. On the accession of Henry VIII., More, together with his father, was immediately restored to office, and rose rapidly to eminence in his profession. So highly was he esteemed, that we are told "there was in none of the Prince's courts of the laws of this realm any matter of importance in controversy wherein he was not with the one party of counsel." He now obtained with ease not less than £400 a year, a very handsome income, being probably equivalent to £4000 or £5000 a year at the present day. He is said to have so scrupulously adhered to abstract justice, that he would not undertake a cause about which he had any doubts, whatever advantages it offered or opportunity for the display of his talents; assuring the client that he would not undertake what he believed to be a wrongful cause for all the wealth in the world. It is not to be wondered at that one who acted upon such exalted principles, and who was known to be a liberal friend to the interests of the people at large, should become popular. In short, by his probity and ability he seems to have reached the summit of his forensic reputation.

DOMESTIC LIFE.

It is by the home life of a man we judge of his true character; and none will better stand this test than Sir Thomas More. Happily, we have the minutest account of his domestic *ménage* given by eye-witnesses; and what they have omitted to tell is supplied by his own simple and charming letters. We have seen him early and happily married. There was nothing to overshadow the bright sunshine of the first few years of his conjugal bliss. But it was a short-lived joy, for he early lost his wife, Jane Colt, who died, leaving him an infant family of one son and three daughters.

Hard pressed with public and private business, he soon found it necessary to marry again; and he was principally desirous to secure a trusty manager of his large household. Such an one he thought he had discovered in Mistress Alice Middleton, a widow, some years older than himself, by no means handsome, and, it is to be feared, not of the most accommodating temper. Erasmus, who was often a guest in the family, describes her as a keen and watchful manager, and careful over her step-children, and with whom her husband lived with as much kindness and consideration as though she had been fair and young: "None ever gained so much obedience from a wife by authority and severity, as he did by gentleness and pleasantry. Though verging on old age, and not of a yielding temper, he prevailed on her to take lessons on the lute, the cithara, the viol, the monochord, and the flute, which she daily practised to him."

Some of their conjugal dialogues have been recorded

by members of the family, from which it would appear they now and then had their little tiffs like other people. She was always for thrift, and looked after the minutiæ of her housekeeping, while he would jokingly tell her "she was penny-wise and pound-foolish;" to which she would retort by scolding him for his want of ambition, and because he had no mind to put himself forward in the world, saying, "Tillie vallie! tillie vallie! will you sit and make goslings in the ashes? My mother often told me it is better to rule than to be ruled." "In truth, good wife," he responded, "you have learned that lesson well; for I never found you yet too willing to be ruled."

As he advanced in life, he gathered around him a very numerous household; for, when his daughters grew up, they married, and they, with their husbands and children, all resided under his roof, one united and happy family, which he governed with such wisdom and loving discretion, that it was untroubled by jealousies or discussions.

We are told it was his daily custom, after his private devotions, "to say the seven psalms, the litany and the suffrages following;" and in the same manner with his wife and children and household nightly, before he went to bed, to go into his chapel, and there to say prayers and collects with them. Erasmus says you might have fancied yourself in the academy of Plato, or rather, it would be more correct to call his house a school and exercise of the Christian religion. All its inhabitants, male or female, applied their leisure to liberal studies and profitable reading, although piety was their first care. No wrangling or angry words were heard there; no one was idle; each did his duty properly and with a cheerful readiness.

But the most charming picture of More as a private man is carelessly sketched by himself in a hurried Latin letter to his friend, Peter Giles of Antwerp, lamenting the little time he could devote to literary composition; "for while in pleading, in hearing, in deciding causes, or composing disputes as an arbitrator, in waiting on some men about business, and on others out of respect, the greatest part of the day is spent on other men's affairs, the remainder of it must be given to my family at home; so that I can reserve no part to myself, that is, to study. I must gossip with my wife, and chat with my children, and find something to say to my servants; for all these things I reckon a part of my business, unless I were to become a stranger in my own house; for with whomsoever either nature or choice or chance has engaged a man in any relation of life, he must endeavour to make himself as acceptable to them as he possibly can. In such occupations as these, days, months, and years slip away. In short, all the time which I can gain to myself is that which I steal from my sleep and my meals; and because that is not much, I have made but a slow progress."

Such, indeed, was the sweetness of his temper, that his son-in-law, Roper, who lived in his house for sixteen years, assures us that never, during that whole time, did he see his countenance clouded, or hear his voice raised in anger. In educating his children he seems to have used the greatest care, especially in giving his daughters such instruction as should make them fit companions for men of eminence in learning and ability. His ideas as to the teaching of women are a decisive proof of his superiority to the notions then prevalent. He resolved to make the ladies of his family learned, sensible, and accomplished. For this purpose he secured the best tutors, and furnished his establishment with ample resources of all kinds—a noble library, a museum of natural history, astronomical apparatus, and musical instruments, with extensive gardens admirably laid out.

A few of his letters to his children, during his occasional absences, have been preserved; they are models of parental love and wisdom. Here is one, addressed to "His whole School." "You see what a device I have found to spare the trouble of writing all your names. Had I named one I must have named all, you are so dear to me. Yet there is no appellation I love better than that of scholar; the tie of learning seems almost to bind me to you more powerfully than even that of nature. I am ready to envy you the happiness of having so many and such excellent masters. I hear, from Mr. Nicholas, that you are, with his help, making such prodigious progress in astronomy as not only to know the Pole Star and the Dog, and such common constellations, but even, with a skill which bespeaks truly accomplished astronomers, to be able to discover the sun from the moon! Go on, then, with this new and wonderful science, by which you may ascend to the stars; and while you diligently consider them with your eyes, let this holy season raise your minds also to heaven, lest, while your eyes are lifted to the skies, your souls should grovel among the brutes. Adieu, my dearest children."

Here is yet another, addressed, "Thomas More to Margaret, Elizabeth, Cecilia, his beloved daughters.—I cannot express, my sweet girls, the exquisite pleasure I received from your charming letters, so much does my affection endear your writings to me, and happily, these need nothing beyond their intrinsic merit, their pleasantry, and elegant Latin to render them agreeable. Nor am I less gratified to find, that, though you are upon a tour, and frequently changing your residence, you omit none of your accustomed exercises. Now, indeed, I believe that you love me, since you do in my absence what you know would give me the greatest pleasure if I were present. Believe me, there is nothing more refreshes me amidst the fatigues of business, than when I read what has been written by you. Were it not for this evidence, I might suspect your teacher of being led astray by his affections in his flattering account of your progress. As it is, I am most anxious to return home to you. Adieu, my dearest girls."

At another time, he urges them to write more at large, saying, "As to the want of matter, how can that ever be felt when you write to me? To me, who am gratified to hear either of your studies or amusements, who shall be pleased to hear you, at great length, inform me that you have nothing at all to say; which certainly must be a very easy task, especially for women, who are said to be always most fluent upon nothing!"

The progress made by these young people quite answered their loving father's expectations. The son was not gifted with much ability, but he was docile and amiable. The daughters were well-informed and accomplished; and his eldest and favourite, Margaret, by her talents and devoted attachment, became the very pride and joy of his heart. We do not wonder that his children were dutiful and good, when we hear him warning them against pride and vanity, urging them to be humble and modest, to "look without emotion on the glare of gold," and not to sigh after worldly vanities, to account virtue their chief good and learning the second, ever remembering the highest wisdom is piety towards God and benevolence towards all men.

A pleasant picture is drawn of More's deportment on Sundays, while he was Lord Chancellor. Instead of imitating his predecessor's parade, he walked with his family to the parish church at Chelsea, and there, putting on a surplice, sang with the choristers at matins and high mass. It happened, one day, that the Duke of Norfolk, coming to Chelsea to dine with him, found him at church thus engaged. As they walked home together arm-in-arm, after service, the Duke exclaimed, "My Lord Chancellor a parish clerk! a parish clerk! You dishonour the King and his office." "Nay," he replied, smiling, "your Grace cannot suppose that the King, our master, will be offended with me for serving his Master, or thereby account his office dishonoured."

Another pleasing trait of his character was his dutiful attention to his aged father, Sir John More, who, when nearly ninety years of age, still sat in the Court of King's Bench, whither his son, then Lord Chancellor, regularly went every day during term time, and kneeling, asked and received the old man's blessing before he took his own higher station. About a year after Sir Thomas's elevation, the venerable judge was seized with a mortal illness, during which he was most lovingly attended by his illustrious son, who watched beside his bed, and with tears and fond embraces evinced his filial tenderness and grief.

An amusing anecdote is told by More's great-grandson,

in which we find the Chancellor passing judgment against his lady. One day, as he was sitting in his hall, a beggar woman made her appearance, and began to complain to him that my Lady, his wife, had in her possession a little dog belonging to her, and which she had lost. Forthwith my Lady was sent for, and desired to bring her lap-dog with her, which she did; when Sir Thomas, taking the animal in his hands, bade the beggar woman and his wife go and stand at the further end of the hall, and each of them call the dog. They did as they were told, and immediately the dog, recognising the voice of its true mistress, ran to fawn upon the beggar. The judge straightway awarded the prize to her. The issue of the story was, that Lady More agreed with the beggar to give her "a piece of gold which would well have bought three dogs," and so both parties were satisfied.

One is curious to know whether this little pet spaniel is the same as appears in the well-known picture of Sir Thomas's household by Holbein, a most interesting and characteristic family group, in which are the portraits of John, the father of Sir Thomas, at the age of seventy-six, and of his wife; of Sir Thomas, at the age of fifty, and his wife Alice, aged fifty-seven; of his son John; of Margaret Roper, the eldest daughter, with her two sisters, Elizabeth and Cecilia, and Margaret Giggs, the daughter-in-law; and lastly, Henry Pattison, who filled the office of "fool" or punster in the great man's household. This admirable piece gives one an accurate idea of the appearance and dress of the various individuals represented, and is like taking a peep in upon them, on occasion of a family re-union. There are many distinct portraits of Sir Thomas More which have made his features familiar to all. His great-grandson describes him as of middle height and well proportioned, his complexion pale, his hair of chestnut colour, his eyes gray, and his countenance mild and cheerful. His voice, though not very musical, was clear and distinct; and he enjoyed good health, having been always simple and even abstemious in his diet.

THE CLOSING SCENE.

After dwelling with complacence on the virtues of this admirable man, whose home character contrasts so strikingly with his great elevation and profound knowledge, it is a melancholy task to recall his end. Everybody knows the sad story, and is ready to shed a tear over the sacrifice of such a man to the savage caprice of a tyrant whose favour had dragged him reluctantly from the retirement he so much loved. There is not a deeper stain upon the character of the brutal and odious monarch than his determination to destroy a man whose character was pure and unobtrusive, and whom he had formerly treated on a footing of such intimacy as to visit and dine with him at his Chelsea farm, and even, as Roper informs us, to ascend with him to the house-top to observe the stars and discourse on astronomy. In persecuting him there seems to have been no purpose to serve, yet it was apparently with the sole object of entrapping the scrupulous conscience of his former friend that Henry got a law passed making it high treason to deny the King's supremacy or the illegality of his marriage with Catharine. Not being able to take the oaths required, More was accordingly committed to the Tower and there imprisoned for twelve months before he was brought to trial. His confinement was at first so rigorous that none of his family were permitted to visit him. He longed to see his beloved child, Margaret, who wrote to him in the most touching language, deploring his absence and endeavouring to comfort him. Yet, even she, in common with his whole family, appears not to have sympathized entirely with his conscientious refusal to obey the King's command. Her father, in a tone of deep emotion, wrote to remonstrate with her on this point, assuring her that "none of the terrible things which had happened to him touched him so near or were so grievous to him as that his dearly beloved child, whose judgment he so valued, should labour to persuade him to do what would be contrary to his conscience." Margaret's reply was worthy of herself:—"She submits reverently to his faithful and delectable letter, the faithful messenger of his virtuous mind," and endeavours to rejoice in his victory over all earth-born cares. She subscribes herself, "Your own most loving, obedient daughter and bedeswoman, Margaret Roper, who desires, above all earthly things to be in John Wood's stead, to do you some service."

His poor wife had no such kindred loftiness of soul. When allowed to visit him in the Tower she saluted him in a plain, rude style of remonstrance:—"What! Mr. More, I marvel that you, who have been hitherto accounted a wise man, will now so play the fool as to lie here, in this close, filthy prison, and be content to be shut up thus with mice and rats, when you might be abroad at your liberty, in favour with the King and his Council, if you would but do as the bishops and best learned of the realm have done."

Having patiently heard her out he tried to convince her that it was better to remain in the Tower than to dishonour himself, but all to no purpose; she retired dissatisfied and sorely discomfited.

We must, in justice, recollect, that the worthy woman did all she could to promote his comfort under these afflicting circumstances, and, at a later period of his imprisonment when all his property had been seized, she actually sold her wearing apparel to raise money for the supply of his necessities.

At length, it being found that he was immovable in his determination not to belie his conscience, More was brought to trial, and condemned to death. On leaving the court he was conducted back by water, and arriving at the Tower Wharf a scene awaited him more painful to his feelings than any he had yet passed through. His beloved Margaret, knowing that he must land there, was watching his approach that she might catch a last sight of him and receive his blessing. As soon as he appeared, she rushed forward, and heedless of the guards with their bills and halberds, in the presence of them all, she flung herself on his neck embracing and kissing him, not able to say a word, excepting, "O my father! my father!" He tenderly returned her caress and blessed her, bidding her remember that whatever he suffered it was not without the knowledge and permission of God; therefore she must patiently submit to the Divine will.

After they had parted, she again turned suddenly back and ran to him as before, taking him about the neck and clinging to him with fondest embraces. "A sight which made even the guards to weep and mourn."

After this farewell, More felt that the bitterness of

death was over, and he awaited his execution with serenity and even cheerfulness. The day before he was to suffer he wrote with a piece of coal, the only writing implement now left to him, a farewell letter to his dear Margaret, containing blessings to all his children by name, with a kind remembrance even to her maids. When about to lay his head on the block he encouraged the executioner to do his office boldly, and then desired him "to wait till he had removed his beard, for that had never offended his Highness." One blow put an end to his sufferings and his pleasantries. Some have charged him with levity in uttering such pleasantries at so solemn a moment; but the lofty-minded Addison thus comments upon the occasion:—"The innocent mirth which had been so conspicuous in his life, did not forsake him to the last. His death was of a piece with his life; there was nothing in it new, forced, or affected. He did not look upon the severing of his head from his body as a circumstance which ought to produce any change in the disposition of his mind, and as he died in a fixed and settled hope of immortality, he thought any unusual degree of sorrow and concern improper."

More's body was given to his family for interment;—to strike terror into the multitudes his head stuck on a pole was placed on London Bridge, but the affectionate and courageous Margaret caused it to be taken down, preserved it as a precious relic during her life, and at her death ordered it to be laid with her in the same grave.

II.

Sir Edward Coke.

IF there be—as I hope there is—some young reader of these pages who has set his heart on being one day a great lawyer, I would invite him to ponder, for his encouragement, the following address of the oracle of our municipal jurisprudence. Sir E. Coke had a passionate attachment to his own calling, and was fully convinced that the blessing of Heaven was specially bestowed upon those who followed it. Thus he exhorts the young beginner:—

"For thy comfort and encouragement cast thine eyes upon the sages of the law that have been before thee, and never shalt thou find any that hath excelled in the knowledge of the laws but hath sucked from the breasts of that Divine knowledge, honesty, gravity, and integrity, and, by the goodness of God, hath obtained a greater blessing and ornament than any other profession to their family and posterity. It is an undoubted truth that the just shall flourish as the palm tree, and spread abroad as the cedars of Lebanus. Hitherto I never saw any man of a loose and lawless life attain to any sound and perfect knowledge of the said laws; and, on the other side, I never saw any man of excellent judgment in the laws, but was withal (being taught by such a master) honest, faithful, and virtuous."

Such testimony, coming from such a quarter, carries weight; and if it be in some measure an exaggerated picture, it has, we may be sure, a great deal of sober truth. A man who shall truly love good and holy laws must have a heart attuned to the highest and most exalted emotions. To enact with a discerning spirit righteous and equitable laws, is to love one's neighbour as one's self, to lay down a common rule of action between men on good and virtuous principles, and thus to bind them together in bonds of brotherhood. It is very remarkable that the counsel which Jethro gave to Moses for appointing of judges was that, "They should be men of courage and men of truth; fearing God and hating covetousness."

To return to the extract quoted from Sir E. Coke's Second Report;—it is no less true than strange that the *opus magnum* of this great lawyer,—his Commentary on Littleton,—was the fruit of his leisure after he had been tyrannically turned out of office, and was in part written during his imprisonment in the Tower. How strange it seems to us in these happy days of freedom and privilege that, but comparatively a short time ago, there were few public men of note who, in the course of their lives, were not sent as prisoners to the Tower of London.

The offence of Sir Edward was that he made a noble vindication of the privileges of the House of Commons, incurring the frantic wrath of King James I., whom he had before offended by the lofty independence which he displayed as a judge, for which reason he had been dismissed from his office of Chief Justice of the King's

Bench. This was in 1616, and five years later, as Leader of the Opposition in the House of Commons, he moved an Address to the King on the subject of the Prince's proposed match with the Infanta of Spain—which was strongly opposed by the popular party—and the war for the recovery of the Palatinate, which they strongly desired. This drew from Sir Edward a Protestation in vindication of the "liberties, franchises, and privileges of Parliament, the ancient and undoubted birthright of the subjects of England."

Bold man! Full well he knew that he must pay the penalty of such uncourtly demeanour; but he quailed not. On a former occasion, when the attempt had been made to cow his spirit, he replied:—"When the case happens I shall do that which shall be fit for a judge to do." So, at present, regardless of personal ease, though far advanced in years, he refused to yield, and was accordingly committed, with Selden, Prynne, and other leaders of the Opposition. Immediately orders were given for sealing up the locks and doors of his house at Holborn, and of his chambers in the Temple, and for seizing his papers.

What followed, Lord Campbell thus relates:—"The ex-Chief-Justice being carried to the Tower, and lodged in a low room which had once been a kitchen, he found written on the door of it by a wag,—'This room has long wanted a Cook;' and he was soon after complimented in the following distich:—

> 'Jus condere cocus potuit, sed condere jura
> Non potuit; potuit condere jura cocus.'

Instead of being prosecuted for his speeches in the House of Commons, the true ground of his imprisonment, he was examined before the Privy Council on a stale and groundless charge, that he had concealed some depositions taken against the Earl of Somerset;—he was accused of arrogant speeches when Chief-Justice, especially in comparing himself to the Prophet Samuel;—and an information was directed to be filed against him in the Star Chamber respecting the bond for a debt due to the crown, which he had taken from Sir Christopher Hatton. By way of insult, Lord Arundel was sent to him with a message, 'that the King had given him permission to consult with eight of the best learned in the law on his case.' But he returned thanks for the monarch's attention, and said, 'he knew himself to be accounted to have as much skill in the law as any man in England; and therefore needed no such help, nor feared to be judged by the law: he knew his Majesty might easily find a pretence whereby to take away his head; but against this it mattered not what might be said.'—He was detained in confinement nearly eight months, and was so rigorously guarded at first that neither his children nor servants were allowed access to him. But he was, after a time, allowed to send for his law-books—ever his chief delight—and he made considerable progress with his immortal Commentary, which now engrossed all his thoughts."

There are two episodes in the life of Sir E. Coke which cannot fail to interest the young,—his training as a youth, and his carrying the Petition of Right.

The father of this illustrious man, Robert Coke, was descended from a good family which had been settled for many generations in the county of Norfolk. Although possessed of a good property he was brought up to the law, and practised at the bar till his death, which occurred when his only son, Edward, was about twelve years old. The boy was of quick parts, and under the instruction of his mother, learned to read. In later days he used to ascribe the habit of steady application which marked him through life, to her early discipline.

In his tenth year he was sent to the Free Grammar School at Norwich, where he remained seven years, making good progress under the excellent training of Mr. Walter Howe, then the head master. He attained considerable proficiency in classical learning, but, it is said, was more remarkable for memory than imagination.

In his sixteenth year he went to the university, and was admitted a pensioner of Trinity College, Cambridge, in the autumn of 1567. Nothing is recorded as to the course of study which he pursued. It is enough that "he laboured to comprehend and remember what he was taught." In after life he always spoke with gratitude and reverence of his *alma mater*, yet he left college without taking a degree.

The death of his father had left him, at an early age, heir to a handsome fortune, and, had he been so inclined, he might now have resided in his country mansion, and been satisfied to amuse himself with hunting and hawking, and acting as a Justice of the Peace. Happily, his wealth did not prevent him from entering upon the career he was destined to pursue with so much honour, and he determined to tread in his father's steps, who was progressing in his profession when prematurely cut off. In those days the bar was considered a pursuit specially befitting the aristocracy; and, indeed, to start in it required a long and expensive education, which only the higher gentry could afford to give to their sons. Accordingly, it was then by no means unusual to find men born to an ample inheritance, devoting themselves with zeal and industry to the study and practice of jurisprudence. Eager to enter upon the race for riches and honours, young Coke betook himself to London,—"not, like other young men, to finish his education at an Inn of Court, frequenting fencing-schools and theatres,—but with the dogged determination to obtain practice as a barrister, that he might add to his paternal acres, and rise to be a great judge."

"*Per ardua ad alta!*" To attain his object he spared no toil, and was content to submit to a severe discipline. "He began," we are told, "his legal studies at Clifford's Inn, an 'Inn of Chancery,' where, for a year, he was initiated in the doctrine of writs and procedure; and on the 24th of April, 1572, he was entered a student of the Inner Temple, where he was to become familiar with the profoundest mysteries of jurisprudence. He now steadily presevered in a laborious course, of which, in our degenerate age, we can scarcely form a conception. Every morning he rose at three—in the winter season lighting his own fire. He read Braeton, Littleton, the Year Books, and the folio Abridgment of the Law, till the courts met at eight. He then went by water to Westminster and heard cases argued till twelve, when pleas ceased for dinner. After a short repast in the Inner Temple Hall, he attended 'readings' or lectures in the afternoon, and then resumed his private studies till five, or supper time. This meal being ended, the *moots* took place, when difficult questions of law were proposed and discussed,—if the weather was fine, in the garden by the river-side; if it rained, in the covered walks near the Temple Church. Finally, he shut himself up in his chamber, and worked at his common-place book, in which he inserted, under the proper heads, all the legal information he had collected during the day. When nine o'clock struck he retired to bed, that he might have an equal portion of sleep before and after midnight. The Globe and other theatres were rising into repute, but he never would appear at any of them; nor would he indulge in such unprofitable reading as the poems of Lord Surrey or Spenser. When Shakspeare and Ben Jonson came into such fashion, that even 'sad apprentices of the law' occasionally assisted in masques, and wrote prologues, he most steadily eschewed all such amusements; and it is supposed that in the whole course of his life he never saw a play acted, or read a play, or was in company with a player."

Lord Campbell comments upon Sir Edward's name, which was originally spelt Cook; and thinks it probable that it took its origin from the occupation of the founder of the race at the period when surnames were first adopted in England. Be that as it may, it is curious to find his forensic powers first called into exercise when deputed by the students to make a representation to the Benchers of the Inner Temple respecting the bad quality of their *commons* in the hall. After laboriously studying the facts and the law of the case, he clearly proved that the cook had broken his engagement, and was liable to be dismissed. This, according to the phraseology of the day, was called "the Cook's Case," and he was said "to have argued it with so much quickness of penetration and solidity of judgment, that he gave entire satisfaction to the students, and was much admired by the Bench."

According to rule, our young lawyer's name should have been seven years on the books of his society before he could be called to the bar, but so unusual and surpassing was the proficiency he made that the Benchers of the Inner Temple resolved to make an exception in his favour, and on the 20th April, 1578, called him to the bar when he was only of six years' standing. His progress in his profession was surprisingly rapid, and it arose, not from the display of oratory or popular eloquence, but from his deep skill in the art of special pleading. Two years after his call to the bar he was appointed, by the Benchers of the Inner Temple, Reader of Lyon's Inn, an Inn of Chancery under their rule. Here he lectured to students of law and attorneys with much applause, and "so spread forth his fame, that crowds of clients sued to him, for his counsel."

He filled this office three years, and before the end of that time he had placed himself at the very head of his profession by his argument as counsel in "Shelley's Case"—a case, said by Lord Campbell to be the most celebrated one that has ever occurred respecting the law of real property in England. From thenceforward, so long as he remained at the bar, he was employed in all important causes that came on in Westminster Hall.

Wealth now poured in upon him; he received an immense income, and invested his monies in the purchase of land. It is said that the crown became alarmed lest his territories should extend beyond the measure befitting a subject, and the tradition goes in the family that in consequence of a representation from the government that he was monopolizing injuriously all land that came into the market in the county of Norfolk, he asked and obtained leave to purchase "one acre more," whereupon he became proprietor of the great "Castle Acre" estate, of itself equal to all his former domains.

Thus, step by step advancing onward, he attained his thirty-second year, when he made a most advantageous marriage. It is interesting to learn that, while he was handsome in person, he was very neat and careful in dress, a point to which he attached no small importance, for he said that "the neatness of the outward apparel reminds us that all ought to be clean within." A quaint old writer thus describes him:—"The jewel of his mind was put into a fair case, a beautiful body, with comely countenance; a case which he did wipe and keep clean, delighting in good clothes well worn." And this hint should not be thrown away upon the juvenile reader. A careless, untidy appearance is always displeasing, and generally indicative of something amiss or deficient in the character. To say the least, it shows little modesty or regard for the approbation and pleasing of others.

Having thus made the acquaintance of Sir Edward Coke in his young days, let us look at him when age and honours crowned his life. He was in his seventy-seventh year when he fought the great battle for our freedom, and stood firm at the grand crisis of the English Constitution. Had he and the other distinguished patriots associated with him then quailed, it is impossible to calculate the mischief that would have been inflicted upon this nation; but, in spite of the blandishments, the violence, and the craft of the Court of Charles I., he framed and he carried the *Petition of Right*, which contained an ample recognition of the liberties of England, and was subsequently made the basis of that happy settlement which was permanently established at the Revolution in 1688.

Charles I. ascended the throne in 1625, and it was not long before the struggle commenced. The first Parliament of his reign refusing to grant a subsidy until grievances had been inquired into, was abruptly dissolved by the King. Sir E. Coke had plainly spoken his mind,—"He would give £1000 out of his own estate rather than grant any subsidy" under the circumstances. It was easy to dismiss the Parliament, but not so easy to procure supplies; and the Government soon came to a dead stand-still for want of them. There was no alternative but another appeal to the nation. In the mean time an attempt was made to disqualify the chief opposition leaders by making them sheriffs of counties, under the idea that they would thus be disqualified to sit in the House of Commons. Sir E. Coke was appointed Sheriff of Buckinghamshire; but this did not prevent his being returned—without solicitation on his part—as member for his native county of Norfolk. He did not, however, take his seat; for but a few months had elapsed when the same scene was re-enacted, and a dissolution followed.

An interval of nearly two years succeeded, during which the infatuated monarch had recourse to the most obnoxious measures of internal government, as though Parliament were never to assemble again. At length, yielding to necessity, in the year 1628, he once more summoned the great council of the nation.

The session had no sooner opened when, on the first day devoted to business, Sir E. Coke spoke as follows: "Dum tempus habemus bonum operemur. I am absolutely for giving supply to his Majesty; yet with some caution. To tell you of foreign dangers and inbred evils, I will not do it. The State is inclining to a consumption, yet not incurable. I fear not foreign enemies; God send us peace at home. For this disease I will propound remedies: I will seek nothing out of my own head, but from my heart [dear old man!], and out of acts of Parliament. I am not able to fly at all grievances, but only at loans. . . . . The King cannot lawfully tax any by way of loans. I differ from them who would have this of loans go among grievances, for I would have it go alone. I'll begin with a noble record; it cheers me to think of it—26 Edw. III. It is worthy to be written in letters of gold: Loans against the will of the subject are against reason and the franchises of the land, and they desire restitution. What a word is that *franchise!* The lord may tax his villein, high or low; but it is against the franchises of the land for freemen to be taxed but by their consent in parliament." With fixed determination that, before the supply was actually given, there should be an effectual redress of grievances, he framed the famous Petition of Right, which, in the most express and stringent terms, protected the people in all time to come from similar oppressions. "In vain the Attorney-general and other crown lawyers were permitted to argue against the Petition at the bar, as counsel for his Majesty, and to combat its positions and enactments; they were completely refuted by the ex-Chief Justice, who not only had reason on his side, but possessed much more constitutional law and vigour of intellect than any of them, or all of them put together." In vain did the King endeavour, by flattering messages and false assurances, to make them assent to waive the Petition. All would not do; following the lead of their noble chief, the Commons resolved that they would proceed; and the Lords passed the bill, but were prevailed on by the courtiers to add a proviso which would have completely nullified its operation.

Sir E. Coke immediately attacked this "amendment." He said, "This is a matter of great weight. To speak plainly, it will overthrow all our Petition. This is a Petition of Right, granted on acts of Parliament, and the laws which we were born to enjoy. Let us hold our principles according to law. That power which is above the law is not fit for the King to ask or the people to yield. Sooner would I have the prerogative abused and myself lie under it; for though I should suffer, a time would come for the deliverance of the country." Thus nobly urged, the Commons rejected the amendment, and the Lords agreed to their desire, to the great joy of the patriots, and all united in beseeching his Majesty to give his royal assent in due form. By the advice of the Duke of Buckingham, an evasive answer was returned, to the effect that the King would do right according to the laws and statutes of the realm.

In sore wrath and indignation the Commons returned to their chamber, and amid the general excitement

Sir Edward rose to address them; but, overpowered by his emotion, touched to the heart with a sense of the danger which threatened his country, the venerable man sank back into his seat, while the tears flowed down his cheeks.

After a time, having recovered in a measure his self-possession, he proceeded to utter a spirited denunciation of the Duke of Buckingham, whom he upbraided as the author of all the miseries they bewailed. "That man is the grievance of grievances," he said. "Let us set down the causes of all our disasters, and they will all reflect upon him." Whereupon the house resounded with cries of "'Tis he! 'tis he!" The historian Rushworth adds: "This was entertained and answered with a full acclamation of the house; as when one good hound recovers the scent, the rest come in with full cry."

Forthwith the Lords and Commons agreed upon a joint-address to the King, which was delivered to him, sitting on the throne, saying that they did, with unanimous consent, beseech him to give a clear and satisfactory answer to their Petition of Right. The King intimated his assent; and the Petition being read, by his desire the clerk announced in the usual form the royal sanction, and the Petition of Right became a statute of the realm. A significant entry in the Journals states, "When this was done, the Commons gave a great and joyful applause, and his Majesty rose and departed."

This was the last appearance of Sir E. Coke in public. At the close of the session of 1628 his growing infirmities caused him to withdraw into retirement, and he passed the remainder of his days at his estate of Stoke Pogis in

Buckinghamshire. Little is related concerning the manner in which he spent the closing years of his life. The last entry in his note-book, written with his wonted firm and clear hand, records an accident, which was probably the cause of his death, although at first he apprehended no such result: "The 3d of May 1632, riding in the morning in Stoke, between eight and nine o'clock, to take the air, my horse under me had a strange stumble backwards, and fell upon me (being above eighty years old), where my head lighted near to sharp stubbles, and the heavy horse upon me. And yet, by the providence of Almighty God, though I was in the greatest danger, I had not the least hurt, nay, no hurt at all. For Almighty God saith by his prophet David, 'The angel of the Lord tarrieth round about them that fear him, and delivereth them.' *Et nomen Domini benedictum*, for it was His work." Until this accident, he had constantly refused "all dealings with the doctors," and used to give God thanks that "he never gave his body to physic, nor his heart to cruelty, nor his hand to corruption." Somebody having ventured to urge on him the desirableness of medical advice, received a notable rebuff, as is told, in the following lively manner: "Sir E. Coke being now very infirm in body, a friend of his sent him two or three doctors to regulate his health, whom he told that he had never taken physic since he was born, and would not now begin; and that he had now upon him a disease which all the drugs of Asia, the gold of Africa, nor all the doctors of Europe, could cure—old age. He therefore both thanked them and the friend that sent them, and dismissed them nobly with a reward of twenty pieces to each man.

It would seem he had received some internal hurt from his fall, and from this time he was almost entirely confined to the house. Gradually his strength declined, and on the 3d September 1634 he expired, in the eighty-third year of his age, enjoying to the last the full possession of his mental powers, and devoutly uttering with his last breath the prayer, "Thy kingdom come, thy will be done." He was buried in the family burying-place at Titleshall in Norfolk, where a magnificent marble monument has been erected to his memory.

III.

Sir Matthew Hale.

"Immortal Hale! for deep discernment praised
And sound integrity, not more than famed
For sanctity of manners undefiled."

COWPER.

IN the year 1666 an opinion was very prevalent, and indeed spread through the length and breadth of England, that the end of the world would come within that twelvemonth. The times were portentous, and astrologers and students of prophecy broached various opinions which probably assisted the natural propensity of mankind to foretell "the end of things created." Whether this were so or no, certain it is that the notion spread, and possessed to a surprising extent the minds of the people, both in the lower and upper ranks.

It chanced during that summer, while the assizes were being held in one of the towns of the western circuit, that a most terrific storm very suddenly arose. The court was then sitting, and the bench was occupied by Sir M. Hale, at that time Lord Chief Baron. An eminent barrister, who was present, has described the scene. All at once an awful darkness overspread the heavens;

vivid flashes of lightning at intervals irradiated every object in court with a lurid brilliancy startling and terrific. Loud peals of thunder rattled overhead, and the reverberation seemed to shake the very walls of the building. The effect on the assembled crowd was strange and fearful. A general consternation seized all, and each looked with eyes of alarm at his neighbour. Presently a whisper or rumour ran through the assembly that the dread moment had arrived, and the day of judgment was being ushered in by that fierce tumult of the elements! Every one, as by common consent, forgot the business in hand; the counsel rose from their seats, and the whole multitude, in a paroxysm of terror, betook themselves to their knees, and prayed for mercy, believing that "the great and terrible day of the Lord" was at hand.

What a scene must this have been! The narrator, a man of no ordinary resolution and firmness of mind, confessed that he was completely unnerved by it; but chancing to look towards the judicial bench, he perceived the judge unmoved, calm, and self-possessed amidst the general confusion. He continued taking his notes, as though all were proceeding in the usual routine, and by his countenance and deportment it was evident that his thoughts were perfectly composed. From this the barrister drew the conclusion that the great man whom he was observing had his heart so stayed upon God, that no surprise, however sudden, could discompose him; and "he verily believed that, if the world were then really to end, it would have given him no considerable disturbance."

The great and good man of whom we have a passing

glimpse thus given us, was one who, by common consent, cannot easily be rated above his true worth. All the judges and lawyers of England admired him for his skill in law and for his justice; scholars honoured him for his learning; and men of God rejoiced in beholding his reverence for divine things, and his pious and consistent deportment, amidst an age of tumult and changes. By a remarkable providence, he was early in life "startled into thoughtfulness" out of a course of folly and sin. He was born at Alderly in Gloucestershire, on the 1st November 1609, of parents in the middle rank of life. When he was only in his fifth year, he had the misfortune to lose both father and mother; and he became the ward of his kinsman, Mr. Kingscot, a gentleman of ancient family, and a strict Puritan. He was sent to school under the care of a pious clergyman, it being designed to bring him up for the Church; and, in consequence, religious impressions were early made on his mind which were never effaced, although for a time he yielded to the counsel of sinners, and walked in the paths of folly.

In his seventeenth year he was sent to the University, and entered the Magdalen Hall, Oxford, where, for a time, he made great proficiency in his studies. Simple in his attire and decorous in his habits, he was a diligent student, and very regular in his attendance, not only in chapel, but at prayer-meetings in private houses; till a strolling company of actors coming to Oxford, "he was so much corrupted by seeing many plays, that he almost wholly forsook his studies." Suddenly there seemed to be a complete transformation of his character. He became fond of fine clothes, took pleasure in gay company, and being of a robust, powerful frame, he began to excel in all athletic exercises. He also learned fencing, and was soon so expert in handling his weapons that he excelled most of his comrades. We are told that although thus given to dissipation, he remained pure in morals, a strict observer of truth, and upright in all his conduct.

In consequence of this change, the young undergraduate gave up his desire of being a scholar and a divine, and turned his thoughts to soldiering. It chanced that the tutor of his college was going into the Low Countries as chaplain to the renowned Lord Vere, and Hale resolved that he would accompany him, and *trail a pike* in the army of the Prince of Orange. His friends tried to dissuade him from this enterprise, and advised him, if he felt disinclined to the Church, to follow the profession of his father, who had been brought up to the bar. But he answered—

"Tell not us of issue male,
Of simple fee and special tail,
Of feoffments, judgments, bills of sale,
And leases.
Can you discourse of hand-grenadoes,
Of sally-ports and ambuscadoes,
Of counterscarps and palizadoes,
And trenches?"

Providentially these idle and mischievous fancies were scattered by an unexpected series of events. Circumstances arose connected with a lawsuit, involving a part of his estate, which took him to London, and brought him into the society of Serjeant Glanville, an able lawyer, and a man of rare worth, who, discerning the admirable parts of his young client, especially his clearness of intellect and solid judgment, urged him to embrace the study of the law. Happily this counsel was followed, and perhaps in no other profession could this great genius so well have served his generation. Baxter, the beloved divine, who, in after years, enjoyed the friendship of Judge Hale, owed his escape from the clutches of his enemies mainly to his testimony and that of the four judges of the Common Pleas, and he gratefully testified "how large a part of the honour of the government and the peace of the kingdom" consisted in the integrity and worth of those great counsellors of the crown. He adds that his lordship assured him he was fully persuaded by his own acquaintance with them, that "there were as many honest men among lawyers proportionally, as among any profession in England, not excepting divines."

On the 8th November, 1629, Mr. Hale was admitted a member of Lincoln's Inn, and, anxious to make amends for time already lost, he at once brought to bear upon his studies the whole energy of his powerful mind. So intense was his ardour that for a while he laboured at the rate of sixteen hours a day, laying down rules for himself which show that, amidst all his ardour for the acquisition of knowledge, he never forgot his religious duties. But it was some time before he entirely relinquished the company of his worldly associates, and he was in danger of being again drawn into his former idle courses. At length, going one day, with a company of young students to a merry-making at a village near London, one of their number went on drinking to such an excess that he was seized with a violent disorder and became insensible. For a time he was, to all appearance, dead. Appalled and conscience-stricken, Mr. Hale withdrew into a private room, and, closing the door, earnestly prayed God to spare the poor victim of profligacy, begged for pardon on his own account, and solemnly vowed to the Almighty that he would never again enter such company, nor drink a health so long as he lived.

This proved to be the turning-point in his spiritual history. The lesson thus painfully impressed was never forgotten, and he was enabled to keep, in all its integrity, the sacred covenant he had made. From this time his course was steadily onward and upward. It awakens no surprise when we find that the studious pains and exemplary deportment of the young man soon attracted the notice and secured the regard of many distinguished men of his own and other professions. It was his happiness to count among his friends the illustrious Selden, Mr. Vaughan, afterwards Lord Chief Justice of the Common Pleas, and the pious and learned Archbishop Usher. Before long he became the theme of applauding conversation, and was spoken of as likely to *rise.* Bishop Burnet relates a curious incident in point. Once, as he was buying some cloth for a new suit, the draper, with whom he bargained about the price, told him that he should have it for nothing on the condition that he would promise, when he came to be Lord Chief-Justice of England, he would give him one hundred pounds. Of course the offer was declined; but, many years later, they met and recalled this conversation in the time of Charles II., when the law-student had risen to be Chief-Justice, and the draper to be an alderman of London.

In the opinion of one most capable of judging, the young lawyer's professional application must have been remarkable. Before he was called to the bar he had acquired a vast fund of knowledge. "He not only read over and over again all the Year Books and Reports, and law treatises in print, but, visiting the Tower of London, and other antiquarian repositories, he went through a course of records from the earliest times down to his own, and acquired a familiar acquaintance with the state and practice of English jurisprudence during every reign since the foundation of the monarchy. From his readings and researches he composed what he called a *Common-Place Book*, but what may in reality be considered a Corpus Juris, embracing and methodizing all that an English lawyer, on any emergency, could desire to know." So says Lord Campbell, and he adds that Hale did not, like the great bulk of English jurists, confine himself to our municipal law, but studied jurisprudence liberally and on principle, not as a mere money-making trade. He devoted himself to the study of the Roman law, saying that "a man could never understand law as a science so well as seeking it there."

It may be interesting to the young reader to know that there was a custom among the Romans greatly admired by Sir Matthew Hale. It was that their jurisconsults were the men of the highest quality, who were trained to be capable of the chief employments in the state; and these men became the great masters of their law. They gave their opinions on all important cases which were brought to them without charge, thinking it beneath them to accept any reward. Indeed they were the only true lawyers among the Romans, and their rules were of such high authority as to constitute one class of those materials out of which were compiled the digests under Justinian. On the contrary, the orators, or those who pleaded causes, knew little of the law, and were but popular declaimers, trained up to be expert merely in giving the gloss of rhetoric, to work upon the feelings of their audience. There is a famous story told, in point, about one Servius Sulpitius, who was a celebrated orator; and on a certain occasion, having to take the opinion of one of these great lawyers, he was so ignorant that he could not really understand it. Upon which the jurisconsult reproached him, saying it was a shame for him who was a nobleman, a senator, and a pleader of causes, to be thus ignorant of law. This rebuke touched him so sensibly, that he set about the study with all diligence, and eventually became one of the most learned men in his profession that Rome produced.

Looking for solid fame rather than early profit or notoriety, Hale was not called to the bar till he was in the twenty-eighth year of his age. He was soon in full business, but was at first chiefly employed as a consulting or chamber counsel. He was not naturally eloquent, and his voice was not powerful, so that he was, for some time, thought unfit for jury trials or the Star Chamber practice. When he had to take the lead, he was an enemy to all eloquence or rhetoric in pleading. He always pleaded in few words, and home to the point. As in all the affairs of his life he was ruled by the strictest integrity and love of truth, so he continued to plead with scrupulous attention to the right of the case, and he used to say, "It is as great a dishonour as a man can be capable of to be hired, for a little money, to speak or to act against his conscience." By degrees his merit came to be more fully appreciated, and in the course of a few years he was at the top of his profession. Still he was courteous and unassuming, kindly to his juniors, and ready to do a good turn to those who needed countenance—and one good word from him was of more advantage to a young man than all the favour of the court.

We are not about to dwell upon the eventful history of the days in which Sir Matthew Hale lived, nor to follow him throughout his public life. Amidst a time of unparalleled tumult and excitement he preserved a steady equanimity of spirit, indicative of the *mens sibi conscia recti;* and while, with calm and steadfast soul he gazed on the general turmoil, he seems to have been charmed by the perturbations that prevailed into "quiet thoughts."

After the "Restoration" the flood-gates of iniquity were thrown open, and it was a difficult matter to keep an honest conscience, and to remain unsullied by the defilements that abounded. Yet, none seem to have found a serious charge that could be laid to him, and on all hands he was regarded with respect and veneration, even by men of various parts and interests most opposed to each other. It has been remarked that there is scarcely in history any fact more extraordinary than that the advocate of Strafford, and Laud, and of Charles I. (had leave been given to plead), should have been raised to the bench by Cromwell; and again, that a judge of Cromwell's should not only be reinstated by Charles II., but compelled by him, against his will, to accept of the very highest judicial trust.

He was made Chief Baron of the Exchequer in 1660, and continued in that office for eleven years. He is, says Lord Campbell, "to be considered the most eminent judge who ever filled the office, and we view with admiration and reverence the rules which he laid down for his conduct. They ought to be inscribed in letters of gold on the walls of Westminster Hall, as a lesson to those intrusted with the administration of justice." Accordingly his appointment to this high trust was universally applauded; "all people thought their liberties could not be better deposited than in the hands of one who, as he understood them well, so he had all the justice and courage that so sacred a trust required." Nor were these expectations disappointed. "While Hale sat in the Court of Common Pleas, in the Court of Exchequer, or in the Court of King's Bench, his qualifications as a judge always shone with lustre in the proportion as the occasion called forth their display. He was equally familiar with every branch of English jurisprudence—the criminal code and the civil code, the law of real property and the law of personal property, antiquarian lore and modern practice. He likewise had the advantage, so rare in England, of having studied the Institutes, Pandects, and Code of Justinian, with the best commentaries on those immortal compilations. While free from every other passion, he was constantly actuated by a passion to do justice to all suitors who came before him. He was not only above the suspicion of corruption or undue influence, but he was never led astray by ill-temper, impatience, haste, or a desire to excite admiration."

What can be more delightful than such a picture of justice on the Bench! Would that all our magistrates were formed upon the model of this admirable character! It is said the only complaint that was ever made of him was that he did not despatch matters quick enough; but the great care which he exercised, while it made him slower in deciding causes, had this good effect, that suits tried before him were seldom if ever tried again. Bishop Burnet assures us he was naturally of a quick disposition; but that by self-restraint he subdued this inclination, having taken as his favourite motto *Festina lente*, which he caused to be engraven on the top of his staff as a perpetual memento. He certainly reminds one of those ancient judges whom the sacred writers described as "fearers of God, men of truth, haters of covetousness." He sacredly regarded the business of his profession as a charge given him by the dispensation of God; and he took "much comfort and satisfaction" in his employment. The whole of his deportment indicated a constant remembrance of the Divine presence, and a reference to the will of his Father in heaven.

As a citizen, Sir Matthew gained immense credit, after the fire of London, by sitting many months in Clifford's Inn for the decision of questions touching title and boundary, and the obligation to rebuild. The restoration of the city, one of the marvels of the age, was mainly ascribed to his care in these respects; and for his services on the occasion his portrait was placed in Guildhall, where it is now to be seen. He also received from the Lord Mayor, as his only further recompense, a silver snuff-box.

There is but one lamentable blot upon the character of this most excellent man. The trial of the (so called) witches at Bury St. Edmunds, and the execution of the poor creatures accused of the crime, is still remembered with a shudder. That Sir Matthew should have been so blinded by superstition as to pass the awful sentence with satisfaction, supposing that he was thereby serving the cause of religion, appears incredible, and we can only marvel that such ignorance should have been found combined with so great excellence and learning.

During four years and a half the honoured Chief-Justice of England retained his post; and it might have been anticipated he would have long continued to give the public the benefit of his services. Hitherto he had enjoyed almost uninterrupted health; but, in the autumn of the year 1675, he was attacked by a violent disorder from which he never rallied. His infirmities increased upon him, and a distressing asthma afflicted him day and night. His appearance sufficiently indicated his condition,—"he had death in his lapsed countenance, flesh, and strength." Perceiving that his days were numbered, he resigned his office, and shortly after bade a final adieu to London, retiring to his early home, Alderly, in the hope that he might be revived and cheered by breathing once more his native air.

For a time the scenes of his infancy, and the recollections of his youthful sports, were efficacious in restoring his spirits, but the improvement was but temporary. "As the winter came on, he saw with great joy his deliverance approaching; for, besides his being weary of the world, and his longings for the blessedness of another state, his pains increased so on him, that no patience inferior to his could have borne them without great uneasiness of mind. Yet he expressed to the last such submission to the will of God, and so equal a temper under them, that it was visible then what mighty effects his philosophy and Christianity had on him, in supporting him under such a heavy load."

He continued to enjoy the use of his reason to the last moment; a blessing which he had often earnestly prayed for during his sickness; and when his voice was so sunk that he could not be heard, those who stood by might perceive, by the almost constant lifting up of his eyes and hands that he was still aspiring towards that blessed state of which he was speedily to be possessed. He expired on the 25th December, Christmas day, a season he regarded with especial reverence; a time which he had spent in much spiritual enjoyment, and which was now to be the day of his final deliverance.

He was interred in the churchyard of Alderly, among his ancestors. He used to disapprove the custom of burying in churches as superstitious, saying, "Churches are for the living, churchyards for the dead." He had prepared for himself a simple epitaph, which was inscribed on a plain marble monument, erected to his memory. There was no need of elaborate eulogy or memorial statue to preserve the remembrance of a man who was reverenced in his own time, and has been so ever since, for the example he set of spotless purity and of genuine piety.

IV.

Lord-Keeper Guilford.

COMPARATIVELY little would have been known of Francis North, afterwards Lord-Keeper Guilford, had not his life been chronicled by a friendly "Bozzy," in the shape of a younger brother, who delighted to do him honour, and who has minutely related the history of his distinguished relative in a very singular and characteristic piece of biography. This narrative is highly interesting, both on account of the ardent fraternal affection it evinces, its stores of anecdote concerning contemporary persons and events, and the indescribable naivete of the style. In the slight sketch given in this chapter the very language of the biographer is preserved almost throughout.

Francis North was of noble birth, being the second son of Dudley, Lord North, Baron of Kertling, in Cambridgeshire, and Knight of the Bath. He was born on the 22nd October 1637, and, in his early childhood, was sent to a preparatory school at Isleworth, kept by a master named Wallis, whose wife, a zealous Independent, "used to instruct her babes in the gift of praying by the spirit." "All the scholars," says the biographer, "were made to kneel by a bedside and pray; but this petit spark was too small for that posture, and set upon the bed to kneel with his face to a pillow; and in this exercise they had their direction from her. I have heard his lordship say, that all he could remember of his performance was praying for his distressed brethren in Ireland."

As soon as he was old enough the boy was removed to a school at Bury, under the superintendence of Dr. Steven, "a cavalier master," and after remaining there two or three years he was sent to the University, where he entered as fellow-commoner of St. John's College, Cambridge, on the 8th June, 1653. During his residence there it is said he principally applied himself to mathematics and natural philosophy, in which he made considerable progress. He left alma mater, however, without taking a degree, nor does he appear in any way to have distinguished himself at this stage of his history.

Having made choice of the law as a profession, he was admitted a student of the Middle Temple in November 1655, and there commenced his studies with diligence and success. His brother says, "He used constantly the commons in the hall at noon and at night, and fell into the way of putting cases (as they call it) which much improved him, and he was very good at it, being of a ready apprehension, a nice distinguisher and prompt speaker. He used to say that no man could be a good lawyer that was not a good put-case." He kept a common-place book, which soon became a massive volume, and made himself well acquainted with the Year-books and the elder writers of the law, thinking that one of his profession could not be well grounded without a thorough knowledge of these authorities.

But, for all he was thus attentive to his studies, it was,

says his biographer, "singular and remarkable in him, that together with this he continued to pursue his inquiries into all ingenious arts, history, humanity and languages; whereby he became, not only a good lawyer, but a good historian, politician, mathematician, and I must add, musician in perfection. I have heard him say that if he had not enabled himself by these studies, and particularly, his practice of music upon his base, or lyra viol (which he used to touch, lute-fashion, upon his knees), to divert himself alone, he had never been a lawyer. And, without acquiring a capacity of making a solitary life agreeable, let no man pretend to success in the law."

As before said, it was our young lawyer's constant practice to "common-place" as he read, and thus, we are told "he acquired a very small but legible hand; for, where contracting is the main business," adds his biographer, "it is not well to write, as the fashion now is, uncial or semiuncial letters, to look like pigs' ribs."

For his personal appearance, it is thus described: "He was of low stature, but had an amiable ingenuous aspect, and his conversation was answerable, being ever agreeable to his company. His hair grew to a considerable length, but was hard and stiff, and did not fall, as the rest of the family, which made it bush sometimes, and not without a mixture of red and gray. As to his humour, he was free from vanity himself, and hated it in others. His youthful habits were never gay and topping the mode, like other inns of court gentlemen, but always plain and clean, and showed somewhat of firmness or solidity beyond his age. . . . . I believe a more shame-faced creature than he was never came into the world; he could scarce bear the being seen in any public places, and when he was student, and ate in the Temple hall, if he saw any company there he waited till others came, behind whom, as he entered, he might be shaded, for it was death to him to walk up alone in open view."

While a student he was frequently in the country visiting his grandfather, who made him a small allowance, and liked to have the lad's company, although he seems to have behaved in a capricious and tyrannical manner to him. "His entertainments at such times were—as usual with gentlemen cadets of noble families in the country—sporting on horseback, for which there was opportunity enough at his grandfather's house, where was a very large and well-stocked deer-park, and at least twice a week in the season, there was killing of deer. The method then was for the keeper, with a large cross-bow and arrow, to wound the deer, and two or three disciplined hounds pursued till he dropped. There was most of the country sports used there for diverting a large family, as setting, coursing, bowling, and he was in it all; and within doors, backgammon and cards. His most solemn entertainment was music, in which he was not only master but doctor." But, notwithstanding these many temptations to idleness, young Frank was always industrious, and had his books sent down to him by the carrier, spending much of his time in reading and common-placing.

At length on the 28th June, 1661, his time being fully out, he was called to the Bar, and applied himself diligently to practice. For a time he was sorely puzzled to find "ways and means." His father, who had hitherto allowed him £60 per annum, being "hard pinched for supplies towards educating and disposing many younger children"—reduced this small stipend to £50, which together with £20 from his grandfather was the whole amount of his income.

His first step was to look about for "a practising chamber." In order to procure this he raised near £300, and with that sum "bought his life in a corner chamber, one pair of stairs, in Elme Court. A dismal hole for the price; for it was not only dark next the court, but on the back side an high building of the Inner Temple stood within five or six yards of his windows: but yet, some more room, and a large study being gained, he thought himself greatly preferred, and he soon filled his shelves with all the useful books of the law which he wanted. His mother had made a collection of legacies and gifts to him, when very young; and when he first went to the inns of court, she gave him an exact account to the time, cast up with the interest, and paid him the sum total at once; and with that stock, he made out a good student's library."

Being thus settled satisfactorily, he gave himself closely to business, attending the Courts at Westminster and reporting diligently, and when any important cause was to be argued, making a point of being present, especially when Sir Matthew Hale presided in the common pleas. It is related that very early in Mr. North's career, when he found it difficult to get to his place in a very crowded court, Sir Matthew said from the bench: "Good people, make way for this little gentleman; he will soon make way for himself." For some time, however, he had great difficulty in keeping free from debt, and he often declared that "if he had been sure of a hundred pounds a year he had never been a lawyer." Indeed, his health began to suffer from anxiety, and from "obliging himself to that spider-kind of life which a young lawyer leads in his chamber," nor did he wholly recover "until a deluge of business drowned all such kind of thoughts."

Happily for this nervous young barrister, he was soon much noticed and encouraged by Sir Geoffrey Palmer, who was made Attorney-General on the restoration of Charles II., and whose son, a very promising youth and the intimate friend of Francis North, died about this time in his arms, having been his chosen companion at college. Thus patronized, he soon began to find himself engaged in practice, and stepped into the business which had been destined for the deceased youth, Sir Geoffrey rapidly bringing him forward by employing him in various matters pertaining to the court.

The first opportunity which Mr. North had of distinguishing himself in public was in arguing the writ of error, brought on the conviction of Hollis and the other five members in the reign of Charles I. On this occasion he volunteered to argue on the king's side, and, although he was unsuccessful, his fortune was made. The Duke of York inquired "who that young gentleman was that had argued so well," and being told that he was the younger son of the Lord North, and, "what was rare among young lawyers, of loyal principles," undertook to encourage him by getting the king to appoint him one of his majesty's counsel. Jealous of the distinction thus conferred upon so young a man the benchers of the Middle Temple refused to call him to the bench, in consequence of which he complained to certain of the judges, who, upon the appearance of some of the benchers in court, administered a severe rebuke to them, upon which he was forthwith elected to their society on the 5th June 1668.

The circuit selected by Mr. North was the Norfolk, where his family interest lay. At first he did not receive much encouragement, but he determined to persevere, "knowing success in circuit business to be a cardinal ingredient in a lawyer's good fortune." This kinsman very naively tells how craftily he managed to make his way, being "exceeding careful to keep fair with the cocks of the circuit and particularly with Serjeant Earl, who had almost a monopoly."

To accommodate himself to the humours of his superiors, and to court their favour, he found the most secure means of advancing his ends, and, accordingly, when concerned as counsel "he stood in great awe of the chief practisers, who, having the conduct of the cause, take it ill if a young man blurts out anything, though possibly to the purpose, because it seems to top them; therefore, when he thought he had a significant point to offer, he first acquainted the foreman with it, which was commonly well taken, and in return he would say, *move it yourself*, and then he seconded it." The biographer further adds, "In circuit practice there is need of an exquisite knowledge of the judge's humour, as well as his learning and ability to try causes; and he, North, was a wonderful artist at watching a judge's tendency, to make it serve his turn, and yet never failed to pay the greatest regard and deference to his opinion: for so they get credit, because the judge, for the most part, *thinks that person the best lawyer that respects most his opinion.*"

Alas, for the morality of the bench when such things were patent to the view of a young aspirant for fame and fortune, and no marvel if the taint spread from the higher to the lower. By such means, joined to a constant diligence and attention to business, the practice of North gradually increased, and some appointments which he received shortly after he was called to the bar contributed to extend his reputation. He was put into the commission for draining the fens; constituted judge of Ely, and made one of the king's counsel before the justices in eyre. Before many years had passed, he became one of the most rising men in Westminster Hall. His mode of life at this period is thus sketched by his brother:—

"His lordship's course of business, while he was in great business, was most philosophical, till he was Solicitor-General and married, and then he kept house, and at meals scarce ever failed his family; but before, he used the commons in the hall at dinner personally and at night in his chamber. And when he was out of commons, the cook usually provided his meals; but at night he desired the company of some known and ingenious friends, to join in a costelet and a salad at Chattelin's, where a bottle of wine sufficed, and the company dressed their own feast, that consisted in friendly and agreeable conversation.

"When his practice was but little, and for the most part, when he was a student, he made it a rule not to leave his chamber before eight at night; and if he had no appointed company, he hath often taken me to walk with him about in the gardens till bed-time; for he never loved at such times to be alone, but having any company, he could discharge his thoughts by discourse. After he was of the king's counsel he kept a coach, and at leisure times used to air himself in that, but with a friend to receive his discourse and give handles for more. But while I was with him, which was first while Sir Geoffrey Palmer was just alive, I cannot say I ever knew him to have been twice at any tavern."[1]

Upon the death of the Attorney-General, interest was made by Mr. North's friends to procure for him the vacant office; and a few months after, he was appointed Solicitor-General, and according to custom was knighted. From this time he practised in the Court of Chancery, and ultimately entirely discontinued his attendance in the King's Bench. So propitious an advancement in his profession, and consequent increase of fortune, inclined him to enter upon a matrimonial project, as "he had now dismissed all fears of the lean wolf," and inclined to take to himself a wife. To this he was prompted by wish for companionship; he thought, too, it "would be an ease to his mind to know continually, after his business was done, what was to become of him, and that he thought best provided for by a family and house-keeping, which is never well settled without a mistress as well as the master of a family. These considerations induced him to look out for a suitable match." He was, however, as cautious and keen for the main chance in this matter, as in the pursuit of business.

"That which sat hardest upon his spirits was, how he should give a fair answer to the question, 'What jointure and settlement?' He used to own but one rood of ground in the world that yielded him any profit, which was Westminster Hall; a meagre particular, unless he might have added, as Finch did, his bar gown £20,000.

There came to him a recommendation of a lady, who was the only daughter of an old usurer of Gray's Inn, supposed to be a good fortune in present, for her father was rich, but after his death to become worth nobody knew what. His lordship got a sight of the lady, and did not dislike her; thereupon he made the old man a visit, and a proposal of himself to marry his daughter. There appeared no symptoms of discouragement; but only the old gentleman asked him what estate his father intended to settle on him. This was an inauspicious question, for it was plain that the family had not estate enough for a lordship, and none could be to spare for him. Therefore he said to his worship only, that when he would please to declare what portion he intended to give his daughter, he would write to his father, and make him acquainted with the answer; and so they parted, his lordship glad of the escape, and resolved to give that affair a final discharge, and never to come near that terrible old fellow any more!"

His lordship's next amour was with "a flourishing widow, and very rich." This lady was closely besieged by lovers, there being no fewer than five suitors dancing attendance upon her at one time. "She held them in hand," says the narrative, "giving no definitive answer to any of them, till she cut the thread; and after a clancular proceeding and match with a jolly knight of a good estate, she dropped them all at once, and so did herself and them justice. As to his lordship, the unhappiness was, he could never find out her resolution concerning himself, and he was held at the long-saw for above a month, doing his duty as well as he might, and that was but clumsily, for he neither dressed nor danced, when his rivals were adroit at both; and the lady used to shuffle her favours among them affectedly, and on purpose to mortify his lordship, and at the same time be as civil to him, with like purpose to mortify them; and his lordship was not so mystified by his amour as not to discern these arts. It was very grievous to him, that had his thoughts upon his clients' concerns, which came in thick upon him, to be held in a course of bo-peep play with a crafty widow. And I have heard him say that he never was in all his life more rejoiced than when he was told that madam was married, whereby he was escaped from a miserable confinement."

Strange to say, notwithstanding his ill-fortune in both these essays, he returned again to the charge; and this time he made his advances to the daughter of a city broker, who had many daughters, reputed beauties, and the fortune was to be £6000. "His lordship went and dined with the alderman, and liked the lady, who (as the way is) was dressed out for a muster. And, coming to treat, the portion shrank to £5000; and upon that his lordship parted, but was not gone far before Mr. Broker (following) came to him and said, £300 more would be given at the birth of the first child. But that would not do, for his lordship hated such screwing. (!) Not long after his lordship was made the King's Solicitor-general, and then the broker came again, with the offer of £10,000. No! his lordship said, after such usage, he would not proceed if he might have £20,000. So that affair ended, and his mind was once more settled in tranquillity."

At length his good mother came to his aid in this perplexing matter, and found him a match to his mind, in the Lady Frances Pope, one of the daughters and co-heirs of the Earl of Down, who lived at Wroxton in Oxfordshire, and had fortunes of £15,000 a piece. On his part, having "mustered what sum of money he could, in order to make an honourable proposition" (which was but £6000), he ventured to present himself as a suitor to the lady and her family, and quickly obtaining the fair one's consent, the necessary writings being sealed, the lovers were happily married in Wroxton Church. There was a great deal of "feasting and jollity" upon the occasion, in the country round about; and the visits, invitations, and rejoicings were kept up with so much spirit, that it was full three weeks, says his biographer, before the bridegroom could clear himself of these well-intended importunities; but "at length we decamped for London, and his lordship took first lodging, and then a house, and lived, consistent with his business, in a way most agreeable to him."

A few happy years followed upon his marriage, during which, as we are told, he was in the height of all the felicity his nature was capable of. He had a seat in St. Dunstan's Church appropriated to him, and constantly kept the church in the mornings. He had the esteem of the royal family, and of all the loyal and conformable people in the nation. His house was to his mind; and having (with leave) a door into Serjeants' Inn Gardens, he passed daily with ease to his chambers, dedicated to business and study. His friends he enjoyed at home, but formal visitants and politicians often found him out at his chambers.

On the promotion of Sir H. Finch to the woolsack, Sir Francis succeeded him as Attorney-General; and his practice, which had before been very considerable, now largely increased; insomuch that, if we may credit his biographer, "it flowed upon him like an *orage*, enough to overset one that had not extraordinary readiness in business. His skull-caps (which he had formerly worn for his health's sake) were now destined to lie in a drawer, to receive the money that came in by fees. One had the gold, another the crowns and half-crowns, and another the smaller money. When these vessels were full, they were committed to his friend (the biographer), who was constantly near him, to tell out the cash, and put it into bags according to the contents; and so they went to his treasurers, Blanchard and Child, goldsmiths, Temple Bar.

This was the busiest time of his life; but even then he neglected no opportunity of attending to his more liberal studies, and acquired a general knowledge of the modern languages. He even made some progress in the study of the Dutch language, to which he was induced by his friend, Sir Peter Lely, "who told him what sumptuous libraries they had, and magnified the elegance and significancy of his country dialect." At the same time he was as diligent a student of his professional lore as ever, noting down in his "solemn common-place book" every matter of importance, and making a copious index of any valuable treatise in MS. that fell in his way. To preserve his knowledge of real property law, he was accustomed every Christmas to peruse Littleton's tenures.

Upon the death of Sir John Vaughan, the Chief Justice of the Common Pleas, in 1675, Sir Francis North was promoted to the vacant office, which he retained nearly eight years. This change procured him a considerable degree of ease and leisure, although at a pecuniary sacrifice—his profits as Attorney-General being about £7000 per annum, while the officc of Chief-Justice did not exceed £4000. During the earlier period of this appointment, we are told that he mixed little in politics, and devoting himself to his judicial duties, discharged them creditably. He applied his attention especially to the reformation of the abuses which existed in the law. One of his proposals was a general register for lands, a scheme upon which, says his brother, "he worked sincerely;" and he adds that the first idea of the statute of frauds proceeded from him. When presiding at the trial of causes as Chief-Justice, he exerted himself to confine the counsel to the point in question, and to cut down that redundancy of speech which, as he said, "disturbed the order of his thoughts." He was, we are told, "very good at waylaying the craft of counsel, for he, as they say, had been in the oven himself, and knew where to look for the pasty." Upon one trying and difficult occasion he acquitted himself in a manner deserving the highest commendation. "At Taunton Dean," says Roger North, "he was forced to try an old man for a wizard; and for the curiosity of observing the state of a male witch or wizard, I attended in the court, and sat near where the poor man stood. The evidence against him was the having bewitched a girl of about thirteen years old; for she had strange and unaccountable fits, and used to cry out upon him, and spit out of her mouth straight pins; and whenever the man was brought near her, she fell in these fits. His lordship wondered at the straight pins, which could not be so well couched in the mouth as crooked ones, for such only used to be spit out by people bewitched. He examined the witnesses very tenderly and carefully, and so as none could collect what his opinion was, for he was fearful of the jurymen's precipitancy if he gave them any offence. When the poor man was told he must answer for himself, he entered upon a defence as orderly and well-expressed as I ever heard spoke by any man, counsel or other; and if the Attorney-General had been his advocate, I am sure he could not have done it more sensibly. The sum of it was malice, threatening, and circumstances of imposture in the girl, to which matters he called his witnesses, and they were heard. After this was done, the judge was not satisfied to direct the jury before the imposture was fully proved, but studied and beat the bush, while asking questions as he thought proper. At length he turned to the justice of peace that committed the man, and, 'Sir,' said he, 'pray, will you ingenuously declare your thoughts, if you have any, touching these straight pins which the girl spit, for you saw her in her fits?'—'Then, my lord,' said he, 'since your worship demands it, I must needs say I think the girl, doubling herself in a fit as convulsed, bent her head down close to her stomacher, and with her mouth took pins out of the edge of that, then, righting herself a little, spit them into some bystanders' hands.' This cast an universal satisfaction upon the minds of the whole audience, and the man was acquitted. As the judge went down stairs out of the court, a hideous old woman cried, 'God bless your worship!'—'What's the matter, good woman?' said the judge.—'My Lord,' said she, 'forty years ago they would have hanged me for a witch, and they could not; and now they would have hanged my poor son!'"

It would have been well for the reputation of Sir Francis North had he always proved himself thus the friend of justice and humanity, but unhappily such was not the case. On more than one occasion his conduct upon the bench rendered him the subject of severe and just observation. His character was destitute of elevation, yet he did not, like many in that corrupt age, stain himself by those evil practices which darkened the characters of men like Sunderland and Jefferies. There is nothing, however, like elevation or high-toned feeling about him; he was *mediocre* in ability, and had not those loftier principles which raise men above the level of their fellows. Still he ought in justice to be regarded in connection with the state of feeling and the general tone of society in that day; and it should be also remembered that he was, by early training and during all his career, in favour of high Church and State principles, the policy he observed as a statesman being that of the old English Tory.

On the 18th December 1682 Lord-Keeper Finch died, and the Lord Chief-Justice of the Common Pleas was offered the Great Seal. An effort was made by Lord Rochester, the treasurer, to induce him to take the office without the usual allowance or pension from the Crown, but this he fully resolved not to do. He saw clearly that there was none other to whom the Chancellorship could be assigned, and he determined not to be outwitted; to use the quaint expression of Roger North, "his lordship was not a chicken that would peck at shadows," and so he remained firm, and positively declared he would not touch the Great Seal without an adequate pension. Ultimately a compromise was made, and he agreed to receive £2000 a year instead of £4000 a year assigned to his predecessor. When the king put into his hands the purse containing the Seal, he uttered this warning sentence,—"Here, my Lord, take it; you will find it heavy." "Thus," says Roger North, "his Majesty acted the *prophet* as well as the *king*, for shortly before his lordship's death he declared that *since he had the Seal he had not enjoyed one easy and contented minute.*" Upon taking his seat in the Court of Chancery, the Lord-Keeper applied himself very assiduously to the reformation of abuses, so far as lay in his power. He expressed himself strongly moved by a sense of the excessive charges and delays of the court, which he desired to remedy. But the variety of opposing interests rendered this a difficult task, yet some progress was made, and had he continued to hold the seals a few years longer, he purposed doing more "to assist in purging out the peccant humours of the court." His manner of life at this period is thus described by his brother,—"His lordship's method, with respect to his great employment, was very commendable; for all his time was devoted to the business incumbent on him. He put but very little of it to his own use, and what passed in easy conversation, which was the chief of his pleasures, had still a regard to his employ by inquiring, canvassing, and debating with those of his society such points as concerned the republic. He had no kind of vice or immorality within his walls. His chief remission was in the use of music, of which he commonly took a relish at his going to bed, for which end he had a harpsichord at his bedchamber door, which a friend touched to his voice. But he cared not for a set of masters to consort it with him.

"The mornings were for the most part devoted to the justice seat of the Chancery, either in the court at Westminster or in the cause-room at home, during the usual periods. His house was kept in state and plenty, though not so polite as the court mode was. The nobility and gentry coming to London were frequent at his table; and after a solemn service of tea in a withdrawing room, the company usually left him, and then the cause-room claimed him, and held him in pain with causes and exceptions often till late. He had little time to himself, for he had this infirmity, that he could not bear to make any one wait; but if his servant told him of any person, small or great, that waited without, he could not apply to think of or do anything till he had despatched him. The interval between the business of the day and going to bed was his chief refreshment, for then his most familiar friends came to him, and the time passed merrily enough; then it was that the court spies found access to plumb his most free sentiments, but with small profit, for he had the same face and profession in public as he had in private; they could only discover that he was an honest man. His attendances at Whitehall were chiefly at solemn times, as on Sunday morning to wait on the king to chapel. That was usually a grand assembly of the court, and the great men had opportunity to speak in discourse to the king as he gave them occasion, of which his Majesty was no niggard; and very excellent things said there on the one side and on the other were a high regale to such as had the advantage to stand within hearing. On the week-days, those called council-days always, and sometimes committees of council, required his lordship's attendance, and Thursday was always public; others for private business upon summons." In the vacations, when he could be spared from London, the Lord-Keeper retired to his seat at Wroxton. For some years he likewise rented a villa at Hammersmith for the benefit of his wife's health, but this he gave up shortly after her decease. He had the unhappiness to lose her after they had been married but a few years. She seems to have been an amiable and judicious woman. She found out when her husband had any trouble weighing upon his spirits, and would divert it, saying, "Come, Sir Francis (for so she always styled him), you shall not think; we must talk and be merry, and you shall not look on the fire as you do. I know something troubles you, and I will not have it so." In his private relations the Lord-Keeper was much beloved. Amidst all the toils of office and the distractions of political life he maintained the same affectionate intercourse with his family, sedulously promoting the interests of all its branches, and regarded by them with grateful and admiring devotion. The fervent attachment, approaching to veneration, which his brothers entertained for him, and which is so quaintly yet beautifully expressed by his biographer, bears a striking and unimpeachable testimony to his domestic virtues and excellence.

At the time when the Lord-Keeper accepted office he found an administration with whose views for the most part he concurred; but on the death of Charles II. and the accession of Sunderland and Godolphin, and especially of the noted Chief-Justice Jefferies to the Cabinet, his position became greatly altered; "with the death of this good master and sovereign all his lordship's hopes and joys perished, and the rest of his life, which lasted not long after, was but a slow dying." It soon appeared evident that he would not be allowed to retain the seals and the principles to which he had hitherto adhered. His resistance to the unconstitutional and illegal proceedings of his colleagues brought upon him the displeasure of the court, and at the opening of Parliament, contrary to custom, the Lord-Keeper was not even allowed to prepare the King's speech, nor was he so much as consulted on that which was delivered.

His enemies now triumphed over him, and, says Roger North, "all the artillery of foul mouths was pointed at him, the Earl of Sunderland being at the head of them. To show their intent of fixing some scandal and contempt on him, I shall allege a ridiculous instance or two. . . . . A merchant of Sir D. North's acquaintance had brought over an enormous rhinoceros, to be sold to showmen for profit. It is a noble beast, wonderfully armed by nature for offence, but more for defence, being covered with impenetrable shields, which no weapon could make any impression upon, and a rarity so great that few men in our country have in their whole lives opportunity to see so singular an animal. Sir Dudley accompanied his brother, the Lord-Keeper, to see it at the house of the merchant before it was sold, and they came away exceedingly gratified with the curiosity they had seen. Flying game soon carried an account of the voyage to court, and it is certain that the very next morning a bruit went from thence all over the town, and as factious reports used to run, in a very short time, namely, that his lordship rode upon the rhinoceros, than which a more infantine exploit could not have been fastened upon him. And most people were struck with amazement at it, and divers ran here and there to find out whether it was true or no; and soon after dinner some lords and others came to himself, for the setters of the lie affirmed it positively, as of their own knowledge. That did not give his lordship much disturbance, for he expected no better from his adversaries. But that his friends, intelligent persons who knew him, should believe it, was what roiled him extremely, and much more when they had the face to come to him to know if it were true. I never saw him in such a rage, and to lay about him with affronts as then; for he sent them away with fleas in their ears. And he was seriously angry with his own brother, Sir Dudley, because he did not contradict the lie in sudden and direct terms, but laughed, as taking the question for a banter. . . . And so it passed, and the noble earl (Sunderland), with Jefferies and others of that crew, made merry, and never blushed at the lie of their own making, but valued themselves upon it, as a very good jest."

Thus "little less than derided," his decrees questioned, discountenanced at court, displeased with the evil measures there favoured, harassed and dispirited, he found himself unable to contend with the adverse circumstances by which he was surrounded. He was attacked by a severe illness, which incapacitated him for his duties, and he became perturbed and full of nervous fancies, carrying himself "as one ashamed, or as though he had done ill, and not with that face of authority which he used to wear." To such an extent did this feeling oppress him, that he fancied he looked out of countenance; and when he went into Westminster Hall in the summer time, would carry a nosegay of flowers to hold before his face that people might not notice his dejection. In this melancholy state he determined to resign office, and applied to Lord Rochester to make application with this view to the King. In the meantime he retired to his mansion at Wroxton, where he hoped to find benefit by the advice of the physicians, and in the enjoyment of rest and fresh air. His affectionate brothers did all they could to relieve and comfort his dejected spirits: music was still his chief solace, "and if ever it was a relief to a mind overwhelmed with troubles, it was so with him;" in short, "with various amusements the heavy time, day after day, was got off hand with what satisfaction could be contrived." The patient, however, showed no signs of amendment, and by-and-by was confined to his bed, where he received the sacrament with his relations around him, it being evident he could not live many hours. The agonies of death came upon him, which he perceiving, "desired his friends not to mourn for him," yet he commended an old maid-servant for her good-will, who said, "As long as there is life there is hope." At length he sank into an apathy, "lay down for good and all," and expired on the 5th September 1685, in his forty-eighth year.

At the time of his death the Great Seal was in his custody. Roger North gives us the following highly characteristic account of what was done with it:—"In a few hours after his lordship's eyes were closed and his will known in the family, all the officers of the Seal then in the house (a Six-clerk, under-clerks, waxmen, &c., who had made a good hand of it, being allowed travelling charges out of the hanaper, and yet ate and drank in his lordship's house) after having laid their wise heads together, came in a body to know what the pleasure of the executors was touching the Great Seal, as if that had been a matter in danger of being overlooked. The executors immediately ordered them all to be ready the next morning to go along with it to Windsor, where the King then was; and the state equipage being made ready for the executors themselves, they took the strong box in which the Seal was kept, and that enclosed in a silk bag, which was also sealed with his lordship's seal. Such a sacred thing is that pestiferous lump of metal. The same night they arrived they waited upon the king, who said, 'he heard that his lordship was much mended.' The seal was delivered in the bag into the King's own hand, who took the bag and asked if there was never a purse (of state), and it was answered that none was brought down. The King said no more to them, whereupon the executors retired; and as had long before been projected, the Great Seal was put into Lord Jefferies' hands, with the style of Lord High Chancellor of England. And what effect that transition had upon the state and welfare of England, let the succeeding times speak."

V.

Chief-Justice Holt.

IT was some time in the summer of 1659 that the incident here narrated occurred. A party of gay thoughtless young Oxonians resolved to enjoy a merry excursion, and betook themselves to wandering about the country, playing all sorts of idle pranks. By-and-by their purses were exhausted, and the question arose, how they might procure a fresh supply of the "needful," without which it was certain they must be compelled to give over their rambles, and put an end to the fun. One of them, who was evidently the ringleader, after listening awhile to the proposals of his comrades, exclaimed, "Now, then! here we are come to a place where four roads meet. I propose that we should part company, each taking a different path, and try to make our way singly, every one by the exercise of his own wits." "Agreed!" cried the others, and, after appointing a place of rendezvous at which they were to meet again in a few days, they turned their horses' heads in various directions, and quickly disappeared.

We shall follow the steps of the ringleader, a fine spirited lad of sixteen, just entered a fellow-commoner of Oriel College, and, if report told true, sadly mischievous and prone to folly. As he rode along, he whistled a lively air, and checking the pace of his animal, began to consider how he was to proceed. At the end of an hour's ride he reached the little inn of a straggling village, and putting the best face upon the matter, dismounted, and, bidding the ostler look well to his horse, sauntered into the house, and, with the air of a millionaire, bespoke the best supper and bed the place would afford. The landlady, well pleased to have so promising a customer, bustled about to make the necessary preparations, and left the young gentleman in the meantime to amuse himself as best he might, till supper should be ready. After a glance around the humble room, he went to look out at the window, and seeing nothing to attract him abroad, sauntered into the kitchen. There he found a girl about thirteen years old, shivering with a fit of ague. The young fellow was sad when he looked at the poor little sufferer, and approaching, kindly inquired what ailed her? She told him that she had been ill nearly a year, and that, although her mother had done all she could, and paid several doctors' bills for physic, she was none the better. And so she fell to crying.

Just then, the landlady came in, and in answer to the youth's questions gave him, readily enough, a rather diffuse history of her daughter's malady and her own domestic affairs. She was a widow, and had only this one child, and she declared, what with the badness of the times and the money she had spent in doctoring the poor invalid, she was half ruined. "Doctors!" cried the young collegian—after patiently hearing her out—"I don't wonder the poor girl is so bad. Depend upon it, she'll never get well as long as she is poisoned with physic; but I could soon tell you of a certain cure." And he looked as wise as a young owl. "Bless your heart! you don't say that?" cried the poor woman, while the sick girl, who was listening from her place in the chimney-corner, pricked up her ears, and, wiping her eyes with her apron, ceased to moan and cry.

"Depend upon it, my good woman, your daughter shall never have another fit if you take my advice and act as I shall direct;" and then, leaving them to wonder over the matter, he returned to the parlour, and ate, with a hearty appetite, the meal that awaited him. Which done, he returned to the kitchen, and was heartily welcomed by the widow and her poor little Sally. "And what—if I may ask you, sir," said the good woman, "what is the advice you spoke about just now? If you do really know of anything which would do the poor thing good, it would be a true charity to tell us of it."

After suffering himself to be again urged, the youth declared that he was acquainted with a wonderful charm, which would infallibly cure the ague, and, indeed, every other kind of ailment! He then felt in his pocket, and drew out from it a scrap of parchment, at the same time bidding the landlady fetch him pens and ink. With much ado, he forthwith proceeded to scrawl a few Greek characters upon the parchment, and then, rolling it up, while he muttered some mysterious words in a low tone, he directed that it should be bound upon the girl's wrist, and remain there until she was well.

His directions were implicitly obeyed, and the result was all that he could wish, for Sally passed that night in sound and refreshing sleep. It was evident that the girl had a profound confidence in the efficacy of the wonderful charm, and, as the imagination is one of the most powerful agents both upon mind and body, this was, of itself, no small way toward the cure. From whatever cause, she was quite another creature, and presently began to laugh and chat merrily, to the infinite delight of her mother, who had not seen her do the like for months.

The next day proved warm and bright, and our young scapegrace spent it most enjoyably, in rambling about, in angling—of which he was very fond—and in various ways best known to himself. The next day, and the next, he found amusement, and you may be sure he was feasted with all the dainties mine hostess of the inn could procure. Her chicken roost, her bee-hive, her dairy and orchard, were put in requisition, and nothing seemed to her nice and dainty enough for "the dear, sweet, young gentleman" (as she called him), who had worked such wonders for her poor child. When, on the fourth day, he talked of leaving, she besought him to prolong his stay, and, with great persuasion, she succeeded. He yielded to her wish, and stopped the week out, making the little inn his head-quarters, during all which time there was no return of the ague. At length he prepared to go, and called for his bill, with as much assurance as though his pockets were lined with silver pieces. Instead of complying with this demand, the grateful hostess told him that so far from accepting a stiver of his money she was only sorry she could never pay him as she ought for the surprising cure he had made, and she added: "What would I have given if you had chanced to come in my way sooner! Had I lighted upon you ten months before, it would have saved me a pretty penny. Take your money, sir! No, no; all I can do is to thank and bless you, and may you meet good luck wherever you go, and the widow's blessing go with you."

* * * *

And now, a long lapse occurs in my story. Years many have rolled away, and all is changed. Still the scene is laid in the same county (Oxford), in one of the principal towns. It is the summer assize, and the judges have just commenced their sittings. In the criminal court a cause has been called, and is now about to be heard. As we look at the bar we see a wretched, decrepit, and very old woman, tottering beneath the weight of years, and trembling with terror. And with good reason she is terrified; for she is going to be tried for her life on a charge of witchcraft; and there is but small probability that she will escape, for the general feeling is so strong against the so-called "witches," that a man stands great risk of being deemed an atheist if he venture to question the existence of such a crime, and to declare against the foolish and impious prejudice of the vulgar in this respect.

There is silence in court as the judge takes his place, —a portly dignified personage, approaching his sixtieth year, and one who has acquired the veneration of his contemporaries, as a man of unsullied honour, profound learning, and the most enlightened understanding. He has, moreover, the character for being apt at detecting false pretences of all sorts, and befriending the interests of truth and freedom.

The case proceeds, and the witnesses are called. They give their evidence with great earnestness, and it is plain they have a firm faith in the truth of what they allege against the miserable being they accuse. The principal charge against her is that she has, in her possession, a powerful spell, which enables her to spread diseases among the cattle, or to cure such as were diseased, at her will; and that she had lately been detected in the use of this mysterious implement. "Has anybody seen the charm?" inquired the judge. "Yes! please you, my Lord; and it is now here ready to be produced in the court." The judge immediately directed that it should be handed to him, which was accordingly done,—a dirty ball, wrapped round with several rags, and bound with packthread. These coverings he proceeds carefully to remove, and beneath them he discovers—a piece of parchment, stained and discoloured, and having some scarcely legible characters—which he immediately recognises as his own fabrication!

For a few moments there is a deep silence in court, while every eye is turned upon the judge. The judge remains silent, and covers his face—perchance in prayer. Then, lifting his head, he thus addresses the jury: "Gentlemen,—I must now relate a particular of my life which very ill suits my character and the station in which I sit; but to conceal it would be to aggravate the sinful folly for which I ought to atone, to endanger innocence, and to countenance superstition. This so-called charm, which these poor ignorant people suppose to have the power of life and death, is a senseless scroll which, with my own hand, I wrote, and gave the poor woman, who, for no other reason, stands before me accused of witchcraft." He then related the particulars of the transaction, which produced such an effect upon the minds of the people, that his old landlady was the last person tried for that crime in the county.

This story is told of Chief-Justice Holt, a judge whose memory is still cherished with high veneration, and to whose eminent services, we are assured, may be in no small degree ascribed the stability of the constitutional system, introduced when hereditary right was disregarded in this country, and the dynasty changed. He was of a respectable gentleman's family, and was born in 1642, at Thane, in Oxfordshire. When about sixteen years of age he was sent to Oxford University, but the complaints of his misconduct which reached his father's ears made him determine quickly to remove the youth from a scene of so great temptation. He was accordingly sent to London, and put under suitable care, being required to keep his terms, with a view to his being called to the bar. These wise measures were perfectly successful; his reformation was complete; he gave himself, with the utmost diligence, to the study of the law, and his moral conduct was thenceforward irreproachable. It is certain, says his biographer—Lord Campbell—that the devoted application to business, the unwearied perseverance, and the uniform self-control which characterized Sir John Holt, could only have been the result of a submission to strict discipline in early years. Shortly after he came of age he was called to the bar, but, like many before and since him, he long remained without clients. When at last he was known, business poured upon him very rapidly. This is not wonderful when we learn that "his *mother wit* was equal to his *clergy;*" and that he seemed to be gifted with an instinctive faculty "to distinguish genuine law, applicable to real business, from antiquated rubbish of no real service." He made himself master of all that is useful in our municipal code, and it is evident that he must have thoroughly imbued his mind with the principles of the Roman civil law.

But that for which he is most to be loved and honoured is his love of liberty; which shone conspicuously in all his career. In that troubled age he associated himself with those who were struggling for the great interests of freedom, civil and religious, in our fatherland. In the year 1683 he was counsel for Lord Russell. Unhappily he had no power to serve the interests of the accused, with whom his warmest sympathies were enlisted. He could but look on while the illustrious prisoner, assisted by his heroic wife, vainly defended himself against the chicanery of the counsel for the crown, and the brow-beating of corrupt judges. There is a consolation in the belief that his own merciful and upright demeanour in the seat of justice may in part be ascribed to the horror which this sad tragedy inspired.

Sir John Holt took his seat in the Court of King's Bench in 1689; and so high was his reputation for law, so great satisfaction had he given in dispensing justice, and such the respect in which he was held for his admirable conduct in his professional character, that his appointment was hailed with universal satisfaction. His contemporaries speak of him with enthusiasm, and it is delightful to read the heart-felt praise bestowed on him by his latest biographer. Lord Campbell says that he "ever reasoned logically—appearing at the same time instinctively acquainted with all the feelings of the human heart, and versed by experience in all the ways of mankind." He adds: "During a century and a half this country has been renowned above all others for the pure and enlightened administration of justice, and Holt is the model on which, in England, the judicial character has been formed."

For two things all will hold his memory dear. He had the merit of effectually repealing the Acts against witchcraft, and after his day no helpless woman was in danger of being hanged and burned in England for being old, wrinkled, and paralytic. He was also the first to lay down the doctrine that the *status* of slavery cannot exist in England, and that, as soon as a slave breathes the air of this country, he is free. No wonder the man who thus made Law the handmaid of Right, was beloved and venerated.

He died at the age of sixty-eight, early in the year 1710; and was buried at Redgrave, his estate in Suffolk, where he had spent his vacations as a private gentleman, mixing familiarly with all ranks, and particularly with the most humble. A vast assemblage from the surrounding country flocked to his funeral, impelled by the desire to pay their last respects to one whose face they were to see no more, but whom they were to talk of to their children's children. "They cared little about his political conduct, but they had heard, and they believed, that he was the greatest judge that had appeared on the earth since the time of Daniel, and they knew that he was condescending, kind-hearted, and charitable."

A magnificent monument of white marble was erected over his grave by his brother at the cost of £1500, representing him seated in his judicial robes, under a canopy of state, between the emblematic figures of Justice and Mercy.

I will add, as I think it may amuse the reader, a pleasing anecdote of Chief-Justice Holt, related in Mr. Harford's "Recollections of Wilberforce." Many persons, even of superior education, contract the habit of interlarding their conversation with one or two peculiar phrases without being aware of it. An example of this was this celebrated lawyer, whose perpetually recurring expression was, "Lookie, d'ye see!" An admirer of the Chief-Justice one day said to his nephew, "Your uncle is a great man, but, what a pity it is he can't talk any time together without bringing in, 'Lookie, d'ye see!'" 'I'll break him of it," said the nephew, and the mode he adopted was the following:—Holt had often found fault with the youth for not giving his mind to legal studies. One day the young fellow surprised him not a little by saying, "Well, uncle, I have thought much of your advice, and have been acting upon it so intently as to have versified parts of 'Coke upon Lyttleton;' shall I give you a specimen?" Holt nodded assent, and he proceeded thus:—

"He that is tenant in fee,
Need neither quake nor quiver,
For he hath it, 'Lookie, d'ye see?'
To him and his heirs for ever."

"Ah, you rogue," said the old judge, "I understand you."

VI.

Lord Mansfield.

FOR much of what is known concerning the youth of this eminent personage we are indebted to Lord Campbell, who, with evident delight, traces the progress of his renowned countryman from the cradle to the grave. Fortunately his lordship had access to family records and sources unknown to former biographers, and was thus enabled to throw a great deal of light upon the obscurity of the early annals of a man destined to become Chief-Justice of England, and one of the most renowned judges who ever adorned the bench.

From his pages we learn that William Murray, the fourth son of Andrew, Viscount Stormont, was born near Perth, on the 2d March, 1705, in the ruinous Castle of Scone,—the hereditary abode of his ancestors for many successive generations. His parents, though of noble birth, were poverty-stricken, and found it a difficult matter to provide for their numerous family, numbering in all fourteen children. Strictest economy was essential in their domestic ménage, and, instead of being taught by masters at home, little Willie, so soon as he could say his alphabet, was sent to school at the neighbouring town of Perth, distant a mile and a half from his father's residence, where he remained until his fourteenth year. In after days, when Mr. Solicitor-General Murray was rising into greatness, envious libels were circulated, sarcastically referring to the straitened circumstances of his boyhood, and giving the following description of his school days at Perth:—

"Learning was very cheap in his country, as it might be had for a groat a quarter, so that a lad went two or three miles of a morning to fetch it; and it is very common to see there a boy of *quality* lug along his books to school, and a scrip of oatmeal for his dinner, with a pair of brogues on his feet, and nothing on his legs."

Report says, that Willie Murray, with his hardy fare and scant raiment, proved himself a boy of *quality* in the best sense, giving early indications of the sharp intellect, vigorous power of understanding, and regularity of conduct which subsequently distinguished him. He was almost always *dux*, or leader, of his class; and although, according to the custom of the day, the ancient punishment of the *taws* was administered for even small faults, his palm never showed a blister.

At the age of fourteen he was supposed to have learned all that he could acquire at the Perth Grammar-school, and his parents looked around them with anxiety as to the choice of a profession for the lad. His family were decidedly Jacobite in their political opinions, and his elder brother, James, had associated himself with the fortunes of the exiled Stuarts in their banishment. It was therefore in vain to hope for court favour so long as the House of Hanover reigned, and there was no chance of preferment in the Church. In this perplexity, Lord Stormont consulted his elder son, who urgently advised that William should be sent to Westminster school, where he would be certain to obtain a scholarship, and might probably find the path open to him before long. This plan was accordingly adopted, and the decision was doubtless satisfactory to the boy, who anticipated with delight the novelties of the English metropolis, so much more attractive than the gloomy cloisters of the University of St. Andrews, to which there had been some thought of sending him.

The most thrifty mode of travelling at that time was on horseback; for the solitary coach which performed the journey from the Scottish to the English metropolis occupied ten days in the transit, and was not only tedious and incommodious, but very expensive. It was therefore determined that young Murray should be carried on the back of a "Galloway," or home-bred pony, which was to be sold on his arrival at the great city to help in paying the expenses of his outfit. Accordingly, on the 22d March, 1718, he quitted Edinburgh, after taking a final leave of his parents, neither of whom he ever again beheld.

The history of his migration and settlement is thus narrated in the "Lives of the Chief Justices:"—"His long, but not wearisome, journey was concluded on the 8th of May. He had been consigned to the care of one John Wemyss, an emigrant from Perth, who had settled in London as an apothecary. This canny Scot had been born on the Stormont estate, and was most eager to be of service to any of that family. He did all that was necessary to launch Mr. William in London, by assisting him to sell his horse, by advancing him money and making payments for him, by buying him a sword, two wigs, and proper clothes, by entering him with the head-master of Westminster school, and by settling him at a dame's in Dean's Yard. . . . .

"William was a good boy, and stuck very steadily to his books. His strange dialect at first excited a little mirth among his companions, and they tried to torment him by jokes against his country; but he *showed his blood*, and they were speedily soothed by his agreeable manners, and awed by the solidity of his acquirements.

"At the end of a year he was elected a King's scholar. Beyond his own merits there must have been some powerful interest required to procure this step, for Westminster school was then crowded, and the foundation was much coveted."

This important event was communicated to his family in a letter from Mr. Wemyss, the apothecary, addressed to the Viscountess of Stormont, in which the good man says:—"Your Ladyship no doubt has heard that your son, Mr. William, has not only had merit but good luck to be chosen a Queen's schollar, ffor I can tell your Ladyship that there is favour oftner that prevails against meritt, even in this case as well as in other affairs of the world. Though, give him his due, there can't be a finer youth, or one who minds his business more closely. Your Ladyship sees that he spends a good deall of money. But he won't spend near so much next year," &c.

During the next four years of the young gentleman's career at Westminster school, the following is the only anecdote of him handed down to us:—Lady Kinnoul, in one of the vacations, invited him to her home, where observing him with a pen in his hand and seemingly thoughtful, she asked him if he was writing his theme, and what, in plain English, the theme was. The schoolboy's smart answer rather surprised her ladyship—"What is that to you?" She replied, "How can you be so rude? I asked you very civilly a plain question, and did not expect from a school-boy such a pert answer."—"Indeed, my lady," he replied, "I can only answer once more, *What is that to you?*" In reality the theme was "Quid ad te pertinet."

Favourable mention is made of his diligence and rapid progress in his studies during these years. One of his biographers, after mentioning that the school had never been in a more flourishing condition than at the time when he entered it, that the number of boys amounted to five hundred, and that they enjoyed the advantage of having the most eminent scholars for their daily instructors, adds:—"In the constant competition of talent, to which additional stimulus was thus given, none shone more conspicuous than Murray. It is particularly recorded of him that his superiority was more manifest in the declamations than in any of the other exercises prescribed by the regulations of the school,—a fact not to be overlooked in the history of one who afterwards, as an orator, equalled if not excelled such competitors as it falls to the lot of few nations or ages to possess. His proficiency in classical attainments was almost equally great."

Similar testimony is borne by Bishop Newton, the schoolfellow of Murray, and his "chum;" who says,—"He gave early proof of his uncommon abilities, not so much in his poetry as in his other exercises, and particularly in his declamations, which were sure tokens and prognostics of that eloquence which grew up to such maturity and perfection at the bar and in both Houses of Parliament."

It must have told no little to his honour that, at the election in May, 1723, after a rigorous examination, it was found that William Murray was still "Dux," for he stood the first on the list of the King's scholars who were to be sent on the foundation to Christ Church, Oxford, where he was entered on the 18th June in that year. It was at first intended that the young Oxonian should qualify himself for taking orders in the English Church. He had, indeed, before he left home, expressed a preference for the study of the law; but his wish had been overruled on consideration of the great expenses of a legal education, which were far more than his father could afford. There seemed no alternative but that he should take orders, and in this necessity he acquiesced; having, however, while at Westminster, occasionally visited the great Hall, and listened to the pleadings of the eloquent leaders there, he felt, as he described it, "a *calling*" for the profession of the law which sharpened his regret at being prevented from following the bent of his inclination. After his removal to Oxford, he casually mentioned his disappointment to a schoolfellow, the son of the first Lord Foley. That gentleman, who had amassed a vast fortune by his ingenious inventions in some branch of industrial science, possessed a liberal and enlightened mind, prompting him to value and encourage talent wherever he discovered it. It chanced that, having seen young Murray at his country-house during the holidays, he had been pleased with his conversation, and discovered in him marks of unusual ability. Learning subsequently that, on account of straitened domestic circumstances, this promising young man was about reluctantly to prepare himself for ordination, instead of following the promptings of his genius in the study of the law, he, in a most delicate and generous manner, encouraged him to enter the career for which nature had fitted him, and engaged to supply him with the requisite means of doing so, until the success which he confidently predicted awaited him should enable his protégè to repay the advance with interest. The offer was frankly accepted, and both had reason to rejoice in the happy results of this friendly act.

Having obtained the consent of his family to the proposed arrangement, Murray entered himself of an Inn of Court while he remained an under-graduate at Oxford, where he resided four years, "making all his studies subservient to the profession which of his own liking he had adopted, his energy being doubled from his considering the responsibility which he had incurred by deviating from the beaten track to obscure competence which lay open before him." Although we have no record of the method he pursued in carrying on these studies, there is not wanting abundant evidence that he laboured diligently to acquire those gifts he afterwards exercised so greatly to the admiration of the public, and to the substantial benefit of the suitors in that great court over which he presided for thirty years. Thus says his biographer—"Those who look upon him with admiration as the antagonist of Chatham, and who would rival his fame, should be undeceived if they suppose that oratorical skill is merely the gift of nature, and should know by what laborious efforts it is acquired. He read systematically all that had been written upon the subject, and he made himself familiar with all the ancient orators. Aspiring to be a lawyer and a statesman, Cicero was naturally his chief favourite, and he used to declare that there was not a single oration extant of this illustrious ornament of the forum and the senate-house which he had not, while at Oxford, translated into English, and after an interval, according to the best of his ability retranslated into Latin. He likewise diligently practised original composition both in Latin and English, knowing that there is no other method by which correctness and condensation in extempore speaking can be acquired."*

In short, it is evident that "long before he ever spoke in public, Mr. Murray had reflected long and deeply on the principles of the art in which, with a view to the distant future, he was earnestly endeavouring to improve himself, and that he had been early accustomed to calculate by what means a particular effect is most likely to be produced on the passions or the understandings of a popular assembly."

The next step of the young aspirant was to transfer himself to London, where he took a small set of chambers, three stories high, in Lincoln's Inn, and set himself in good earnest to acquire a knowledge of his profession. Of the course of study which produced the most accomplished judge who ever presided in the court of King's Bench, we have, says his biographer, only an imperfect account, but we know that he owed everything to private and spontaneous exertion. "First, he thoroughly

* "Lives of Chief-Justices."

grounded himself in ancient and modern history by a perusal of the most eminent original historians. He then applied diligently to ethics, which he mastered; and from his own experience he always strongly recommended the philosophical works of Cicero. The foundation of jurisprudence he maintained to be the Roman civil law. Thence he proceeded to international law, doing full justice to the learning and genius of Grotius, its codifier and almost its founder. Next, he entered on the feudal law, without which our law of real property must be very imperfectly understood. Next came the English municipal law, and this he was obliged to search for in very crabbed and uncouth compositions, which often filled him with disgust and sometimes with despair. . . . ."

While by such multifarious and severe studies he was preparing himself to be a great advocate and the prince of judges, by a wise disposition of his time he still mixed in general society and attended to elegant literature. In his life of Johnson, Boswell speaks of Mr. Murray as a young man who was then "drinking champagne with the wits," referring probably to the fact of his intimate friendship with Pope.

"To this prince of poets he had been introduced, while at Westminster school, by his countryman Lord Marchmont, and a warm and steady friendship sprang up between them. The young Scot was at first exceedingly flattered and delighted by the notice of a writer of such celebrity, whose 'Pastorals' he had got by heart when a child, but whom, till he was sent to England, he had never hoped to behold. Afterwards he had the good taste to relish the exquisite powers of conversation which the bard could display in the company of those he liked, and he was touched by experiencing constant kindness from one who was disposed to treat nobles and kings with disdain. Pope, on the other hand, intuitively discovered the genius of this juvenile worshipper, was struck by his extraordinary accomplishments, agreeable manners, and, it is said, above all, by *the silvery tones of his voice*, which seem then and ever after to have doubled the effect of all his other powers to win his way in the world."* In such favour was Murray with his illustrious friend that he had frequent invitations to Pope's villa at Twickenham, and Pope, coming to Lincoln's Inn, would instruct the youthful neophyte in the graces of oratory. It is related that one day a gay Templar having unceremoniously entered Murray's rooms, surprised him in the act of practising before a mirror, while Pope sat by in the character of preceptor. There must have been something unusually prepossessing about the youth who could thus inspire in the fastidious poet a warmth of affection rare indeed to be met with in such a personage; nor did the feeling prove evanescent, but was prolonged till the death of Pope, and its genuineness was evinced by the interchange of all the offices of a generous and true friendship.

After so diligent a preparation we do not wonder to find the young lawyer qualified, when the opportunity presented itself, to shine in the profession for which he had displayed so rooted an attachment. He appears from the first to have formed a settled resolve to attain the highest honours it can confer, and he panted for the lucky moment when he might begin to scale the ladder. For a few years his gains were comparatively small. It

* "Lives of the Chief-Justices."

is a pleasant trait in his character that he dedicated his first professional earnings to the purchase of a set of tea-china, with suitable silver-plate, for his sister-in-law, Lady Stormont, who, after his father's death, had sent him supplies of Scotch marmalade, as well as pecuniary contributions to assist him while he was a student at Lincoln's Inn. It was not long before he began to be engaged in important cases of appeal, and his connections, personal character, and the reputation which he had acquired at the University, all contributed to his success. Yet, in spite of his rising fame, he was unsuccessful in an affair of the heart. The lady of his choice had beauty, accomplishments, and birth for her dower, and listened favourably to his suit, but her friends, from pecuniary considerations, refused their sanction, and married her to a wealthy squire. This disappointment for a time inflicted a deep wound; and Pope endeavoured as best he might to cheer his downcast spirits by addressing to him an imitation of the Sixth Epistle of the First Book of Horace. The following lines have been often quoted:—

> " —— If not so pleased, at council board rejoice
> To see their judgments hang upon thy voice;
> From morn to night, at Senate, Rolls, and Hall,
> Plead much, read more, dine late, or not at all.
> But wherefore all this labour, all this strife,
> For fame, for riches, for a noble wife?
> Shall one whom native learning, birth conspired
> To form, not to admire, but be admired,
> Sigh, while his Chloe, blind to wit and worth,
> Weds the rich dullness of some son of earth?
> Yet time ennobles or degrades each line;
> It brightened Craggs's, and may darken thine—
> And what is fame? the meanest have their day;
> The greatest can but blaze and pass away."

How far the poet's friendly skill availed appears doubtful. But before many months had passed the growing celebrity of Mr. Murray placed him in a position to aspire again after the happiness of wedded life, and this time his suit was urged with success. He married a lady of rank and accomplishments, and one whose love formed the happiness of a long life crowned with honour, and in no small degree beneficial to his fellow-countrymen.

"The great Lord Mansfield" was the epithet by which he was known to the men of his own generation, and few, if any, have excelled him in the peculiar excellencies that most adorn the position he so long filled. Among the numerous tributes paid to his genius, we find the testimonies of some of the wisest and most renowned of his contemporaries. Not only did Pope celebrate him in undying verse, but the gentle Cowper wrote some pleasing stanzas bewailing the outrage committed by the mob at the time of the celebrated riots of 1780, when the house of the venerable Chief-Justice was destroyed by fire, and his invaluable library of books and manuscripts perished in the flames. Lord Mansfield's personal appearance is thus characteristically described by Cowper in a letter to Hayley :—" The monument of Lord M., for which you say Flaxman is engaged, will, I dare say, prove a noble effort of genius. Statuaries, as I have often heard an eminent one say, do not much trouble themselves about likeness, else I would give much to be able to communicate to Flaxman the perfect idea I have of this subject, such as he was forty years ago. He was at that time wonderfully handsome, and would expound the most mysterious intricacies of the law, or recapitulate both matter and evidence of a cause as long as from here to Eartham, with an intelligent smile on his features that bespoke plainly the perfect ease with which he did it. The most abstruse studies, I believe, never cost him any labour." Lord Chesterfield wrote to his son in glowing terms of the rising talents of Mr. Pitt and Mr. Murray: "No man," says he, "can make a figure in this country but by Parliament. Your fate depends on your success as a speaker, and, take my word for it, that success turns much more upon manner than matter. Mr. Pitt, and Mr. Murray, the Solicitor-General, are beyond comparison the best speakers. Why? Only because they are the best orators. They alone can inflame or quiet the House; they alone are attended to in that numerous and noisy assembly, that you might hear a pin fall while either of them is speaking. Is it that their matter is better or their arguments stronger than other people's? Does the House expect extraordinary information from them? Not in the least; but the House expects pleasure from them, and therefore attends; finds it, and therefore approves."

Bishop Hurd, after passing a fine eulogium upon the talents displayed by Lord Mansfield in every department of the State, and more especially "in the Supreme Court of Justice, his peculiar province," adds, "his lordship's public senatorial character much resembled that of Messala, of whom Cicero says, addressing himself to Brutus, that for worth, honour, and a warm love of his country, hardly any one is comparable to Messala, so that his eloquence (in which he wonderfully excels) is almost eclipsed by those virtues; and even in his display of that faculty his superior good sense shows itself most, with so much care and skill hath he formed himself to the truest manner of speaking. His powers of genius and invention are confessedly of the first size, yet he almost owes less to them than to the diligent and studious cultivation of judgment."

Not less eulogistic is Bishop Warburton, who declares that during Lord Mansfield's administration, "the stream of justice ran as pure as from its own celestial source; purer than Plato dared to conceive it, even in his feigned republic." Another admirer writes that his words might be said to "drop manna;" and that, if the bolder metaphor of Anacreon could be anywhere justified, it might be here—that "he spoke roses."

These lively pictures of the individual, drawn by contemporary pens, are usually more effective than those which are traced only from the relation of others. We seem to have, as it were, the features and the tones conveyed to us, together with the language of the orator. Everywhere Lord Mansfield's advent excited a general interest, and men ran eagerly to listen to him, as we read in the memoirs of various writers of the day. Once only was the Midland Circuit honoured by his presence, on which occasion the utmost curiosity was displayed to see and hear him; with what results we learn from the pen of a spectator: "The second judge only arrived with the cavalcade, while the superior stole into Leicester late at night on a saddle-horse. Next morning, however, he appeared in all his splendour, and might justly be pronounced to be Grace and Dignity personified. But when every eye was strained, and every ear attentive, and the crier of the court in due form had proclaimed silence, his lordship only coldly got up and said, that as he was certain the grand jury were so well informed of their duties, he should give no charge, but proceed immediately to the trials. Thus, by complimenting a few, he disobliged the many; and this conduct was the more reprehended, as he was not restricted for time, and could have gratified all without giving himself the least trouble."*

Of the unparalleled ascendency enjoyed by this great judge in Westminster Hall, there are some remarkable proofs on record. One of the most so, perhaps, is the fact that, of the many thousand judgments which he pronounced during the third part of a century, two only were reversed; while, throughout that whole period, there were only two cases in which his opinion was not unanimously adopted by his brethren who sat with him on the bench. No judge, according to Mr. Roscoe, ever impressed so forcibly upon the jurisprudence of this country the peculiar qualities of his own mind, insomuch that "many of the most important branches of modern law derive their character, and almost their existence, from his genius."

I shall conclude this chapter by quoting yet one more passage from Lord Campbell's Memoir of Lord Mansfield, which especially deserves the attention of the young reader. He says:—

"It would be highly instructive, considering his multiplicity of engagements, all of which he fulfilled so admirably, to have learned what were the rules he laid down for the distribution of his time; but we all know —and this should ever be borne in mind by those who would rise to eminence—that he was habitually industrious and habitually temperate. A sentence given him

* "Cradock's Memoirs," vol. i.

as a copy, when he began to learn text-hand at Perth school, was, 'Opere peracto ludemus.' This he used often to repeat in after life, and always to act upon. For example, when the great case of Doe ex Dem. Taylor *v.* Horde was depending, which required a research into some of the most recondite points of the law of real property, he thus wrote to a friend: 'I am very impatient to discharge myself entirely of it. While the company is at cards, I play my rubbers at this work, not the pleasantest in the world; but what must be done, I love to do and have it over.'"

VII.

Sir J. Eardley Wilmot.

"Bread and water are nectar and ambrosia, when contrasted with the supremacy of a court of justice."

STRANGE words these in the mouth of a successful lawyer, and of one, too, who did not, as so many have done, cry "sour grapes." More than once Sir E. Wilmot refused the Great Seal when it was within his grasp; and, throughout his long and prosperous career, he desired nothing so much as to enjoy the luxury of retirement, and to bury himself in the shades of oblivion. "The withdrawing from the eyes of mankind," he said, "has always been my favourite wish; it was the first, and will be the last of my life."

Undoubtedly, and perhaps it may be said happily, such a character is a very rare and exceptional one. The life of a distinguished, yet unambitious lawyer, claims notice on account of its singularity; and it becomes interesting when we find that this eccentricity was combined with excellence of moral character, and the most pure and elevated feelings. This remarkable man was the second son of a respectable country gentleman residing in the neighbourhood of Derby, and his birth took place on the 16th August 1709. He was at first sent to the free school at Derby, and was then placed under the care of the celebrated Mr. Hunter at Litchfield, five of whose pupils afterwards sat together as judges in the superior courts at Westminster. Another renowned scholar trained by the same master was Samuel Johnson, whom Wilmot, when Chief-Justice, used frequently to mention as a "long, lank, lounging boy, whom he distinctly remembered to have been punished by Hunter for idleness." The great lexicographer gave this account of the formidable dominie: "The head-master was very severe, and wrong-headedly severe. He used to beat us unmercifully, and he would beat a boy equally for not knowing a thing as for neglecting to know it. He would call up a boy and ask him Latin for a *candlestick*, which the boy did not expect to be asked. While Hunter was flogging his boys unmercifully, he used to say, 'And this I do to save you from the gallows.'"

It appears that under this harsh discipline the pupils became adepts at their tasks, and were imbued with a love of learning; and it is said Johnson himself had so high an idea of the beneficial effects of such discipline, that when he heard of a schoolmaster having abolished flogging, he exclaimed, "I am afraid what his boys gain at one end they will lose at the other." Another of the illustrious roll-call of Mr. Hunter's pupils was David Garrick, then a very little fellow, sitting on the lowest form, and who, many years afterwards, told the following anecdote of Mr. Wilmot, at the time he was a barrister of well-known eminence. A case of considerable interest had arisen, in which one of the parties, being an old school-fellow, insisted on retaining Wilmot for his counsel; and Garrick, who took a lively interest in the affair, attended in court, placing himself in a snug corner, where he expected to remain unobserved. He thus described what occurred:—

"There appeared much contradiction and confusion in the evidence given by the witnesses, till at length rose Mr. Wilmot, who immediately explained the whole in so clear and animated a manner, as to charm as well as inform every one who heard him. I was delighted with the wit and sprightliness with which he unravelled the whole affair—pluming myself upon being quite private and unnoticed in so great a crowd, and little thinking that I should be soon brought upon the stage myself. But the counsel, having developed the plot which had been laid against his client, observed, 'In short, gentlemen of the jury, it is nothing more than the story of *The Intriguing Chamber-maid*, and *The Lying Varlet*.' [These two farces, written by Garrick, were then acting with great applause.] And, immediately casting his sparkling eye upon me in my retired corner, in a moment he drew the notice of the whole court upon me, and I thought I should have sunk into the earth."

After young Wilmot had passed some years at Litchfield, he was removed to Westminster School, where we learn that he applied himself diligently to his books, but without mixing in the usual sports and associations of his companions. The next few years he spent as a recluse student at Trinity Hall, Cambridge, his desire being to make the Church his profession, in the hope of obtaining some small living, and spending his days in the quiet seclusion of a country parson's life. But to this his father made strenuous objection. "You have," said he, "such talents and acquirements as will qualify you to make a figure in the world, and it is my express desire and earnest wish that you should devote yourself to the study of the law." This parental counsel, urged with the warmth of affection, prevailed over the natural inclination of the dutiful son, and he complied, though with reluctance. Accordingly, before he left Trinity Hall, he was initiated in the Roman civil law; "a study for which," says Lord Campbell, "this place of education has always been renowned, and to which he afterwards ascribed his proficiency in the common law of England."

The young lawyer afterwards kept terms in the Inner Temple, and at the end of three years' residence there, was called to the bar. Nothing is known of his plan of study; the result alone was unquestionable—he rendered himself a consummate jurist. Far, however, from seeking to display his acquirements, he studiously endeavoured to conceal them, lest his familiarity with "black-letter learning" should bring him into favour with the attorneys, and thus force him into notice. For a considerable time he preserved his incognito, and thus secured himself from molestation, avoiding every opportunity of exhibiting his abilities. At length, "arguing some demurrers and new trials in causes from his circuit, he was betrayed to Westminster Hall as a deep lawyer and powerful advocate. Thereupon Sir Dudley Ryder, the Attorney-General, appointed him 'Treasury Devil;'* and deriving important aid from his services, and being very desirous of bringing him forward, mentioned him to the Lord Chancellor, as a man who might be an orna-

* "Treasury Devil," the familiar title of the junior counsel to whose care the legal business of the Government is entrusted.

ment to his profession, and would one day show himself qualified for the highest judicial station." *

Had he been so disposed, he might now—to use the expression of a friend whom he consulted—have "hoisted the sail, sure of a trade-wind." Nothing was further from his wish. In spite of all remonstrances, he resolutely refused to "wear silk," and persisted in declining the rank of King's Serjeant. Nor was he even to be tempted by the offer of a seat in the House of Commons free of expense. This he despised, "equally disliking the notion of making a speech either as a patriot or as a courtier; and the notion suggested to him that Parliament might speedily make him a law officer of the Crown, filled him with consternation." †

At once and finally to escape such perils and solicitations, and bent upon enjoying the delights of retirement and domestic bliss, he determined altogether to abandon Westminster Hall, and settle in his native county as a provincial counsel. Thus, he flattered himself, he should secure the first wish of his heart, and never more be troubled with intrusive alarms of professional advancement. Twelve happy months glided by, and it seemed that he might believe himself forgotten and left in peace. He was happily married to the lady of his choice, and he asked and desired nothing better than to be suffered alone to pursue his unambitious career. Suddenly, however, a report reached him that, in consequence of the death of Sir M. Wright, one of the judges of the Court of King's Bench, his Majesty had been pleased to appoint himself successor to the vacant office. At first he refused to believe this, but an official

* "Lives of the Chief-Justices," vol. ii. p. 282. † *Ibid.*

intimation of the fact put it beyond all doubt; and the reluctant, home-loving, peace-coveting Wilmot was compelled, notwithstanding all his protestations and entreaties, to do his duty, and serve the public cause according to the best of his ability. In Hilary Term 1755 he took his seat as one of the Puisne judges of the King's Bench, and according to custom, was knighted.

In the following year Sir E. Wilmot received another proof of the high esteem in which he was held, when he was appointed one of the Commissioners of the Great Seal, on the resignation of Lord Hardwicke; and so well did he acquit himself in the discharge of the novel duties of this office that there was a general expectation he would soon be appointed Lord Chancellor, an event the possibility of which filled him with apprehension. In a letter to his brother he said, "The acting junior of the commission is a spectre I started at, but the sustaining the office alone I must and will refuse at all events. I will not give up the peace of my mind to any earthly consideration whatever." And to this resolution he adhered when the offer was actually made to him once and again. Shortly after this period, in the year 1757, while presiding at the Worcester assizes, Sir Eardley had a very narrow escape of his life. In a letter to his wife he gave the following account of the occurrence:—

"I send this by express on purpose to prevent your being frightened, in consequence of a most terrible accident. Between two and three, as we were trying causes, a stack of chimneys blew upon the top of that part of the hall where I was sitting, and beat the roof down upon us; but, as I sat close up to the wall, I have escaped without the least hurt. When I saw it begin to yield and open I despaired of my own life and the lives of all within the compass of the roof. Mr. John Lawes is killed, and the attorney in the cause which was trying is killed, and I am afraid some others. It was the most frightful scene I ever beheld. I was just beginning to sum up the evidence to the jury, and intending to go immediately after I had finished. Most of the counsel were gone, and they who remained in court are very little hurt, though they seemed to be in the place of the greatest danger. If I am thus preserved for any good purpose, I rejoice at the event, and both you and the little ones will have reason to join with me in returning God thanks for this signal deliverance; but if I have escaped to lose either my honour or my virtue, I shall think, and you ought to concur with me in thinking, that the escape is my greatest misfortune.

"I desire you will communicate this to my friends, lest the news of such a tragedy, which fame always magnifies, should affect them with fears for me. Two of the jurymen who were trying the cause are killed, and they are carrying dead and wounded bodies out of the ruins still."

In another letter the judge says: "It was an image of the last day, when there shall be no distinction of persons, for my robes did not make way for me. I believe an earthquake arose in the minds of most people, and there was an apprehension of the fall of the whole hall." It is said that he owed his safety to the presence of mind he manifested in remaining quietly in his place till the confusion was over. "His 'mens sana,'" says one to whom he was personally known, "in every position of life always predominated."

For ten years Sir Eardley continued to act as Puisne

Judge of the King's Bench; but he seems to have perpetually sighed after an opportunity of exchanging this situation for one less conspicuous and laborious, and he was meditating some step of the kind when, to his alarm, he found himself summoned to "go up higher;" Lord Camden, then raised to the Chancellorship, having determined that Wilmot should succeed him as Chief-Justice of the Common Pleas. When the intimation of this promotion reached him he wrote imploringly to his brother, saying, "Is it not possible for you to divert a measure which will be so injurious to my peace if accepted, and so much censured if refused?" His brother, who did not share his scruples, replied, "I am clearly of opinion your removal to the Common Pleas will be a fortunate and happy event. Every mortal says how honourable it is for you to have no competitor. Sit but serene in your chief seat, and out of it you may rage like Boreas." There was nothing left but to submit; yet the horror of promotion was so great in the mind of this strangely constituted man that he positively wrote a letter to refuse, with all respect and gratitude, the honour designed him. This he communicated to his friend and colleague Sir Joseph Yates, who, by urgent solicitation and with skilful persuasion, induced him to revoke his determination, and himself sketched a letter of acceptance which he made Sir Eardley sign.

On the evening of the day when the new Chief-Justice "kissed hands" on being appointed, he thus addressed his son, a lad of seventeen, who attended him to his bedside: "Now, my son, I will tell you a secret worth knowing and remembering. The elevation I have met with in life, particularly this last instance of it, has not been owing to any superior merit or abilities, but to my humility—to my not having set myself up above others, and to an uniform endeavour to pass through life void of offence towards God and man."

During four years he continued to fulfil with characteristic good sense and wisdom his judicial office; at length, finding himself, on the death of Lord Chatham, urged to accept the highest place in his profession, and being resolutely fixed not to yield, he resigned his justiceship on the plea of ill-health, and with no other condition than that he should not be pensioned out of the civil list. "I would much rather resign," he wrote, "without any remuneration at all. The *plus* or the *minus* of sufficiency lies only in my own breast. I hate and detest pensions, and hanging upon the public like an almsman."

Being thus relieved from the toils of office, Sir Eardley devoted much of his time to the pursuits in which he had always taken delight. For a considerable time he also continued to hear appeals in the Privy Council, and afterwards devoted himself entirely to the duties and enjoyments of private life. In his own family he was greatly beloved, and the pious hand of his son has memorialized his life in a most pleasing manner. Nothing seems to have solaced and delighted him so much as the society of his domestic circle, and in the formation of his children's character he exercised assiduous care, inculcating in the most affectionate manner the noblest lessons of virtue and honour. His letters to his family have been preserved, and abound in pure and elevated sentiments. Thus he wrote to his son, a boy of fifteen: "I take the first vacant hour I have this month to acknowledge the receipt of your letter, and to assure you of my love and affection. I do not in the least doubt but you will merit them by seconding my endeavours to cultivate your mind, and chiefly to imbue it with those principles of honour and truth which constitute a gentleman, and which I received, in the utmost purity, from my own father, and desire to transmit to you, and your brothers and sisters, as unsullied as I received them; and however fortune may exalt or depress you in the world, the consciousness of having always acted upon those principles will give you the only perfect happiness that is to be found in this world. But, above all things, remember your duty to God, for without his blessing my love and affection for you will be as ineffectual to promote your happiness here as hereafter; and whether my heart be full of joy or grief it will always beat uniformly with unremitting wishes that all my children may be more distinguished for their goodness than for their greatness."

So good a father deserved all the encomiums which were bestowed on him by the voice of filial piety, and Sir E. Wilmot seems to have been greatly beloved and admired by all his associates. None has spoken unkindly of him save Horace Walpole, and his criticisms are so evidently unjust that they have been attributed to the influence of party malignity. His life was prolonged to an advanced age, and he died venerated by his contemporaries and lamented by his friends. An impartial biographer has said of him, that although he never shone as a statesman or an orator, he is to be placed in a very high rank in the order of judges. To the most exemplary patience and purity he joined an unusual store of juridical knowledge, which enabled him to decide with promptitude the various questions of law on which the settlement of each case depended, and to determine them with perfect accuracy.

Although never fond of the practice of law as a profession, Sir E. Wilmot often declared his partiality for the study of it as a science; and, as a proof of this, after he had retired from office, he always bought and read the latest reports, and sometimes borrowed MS. notes from young barristers.

VIII.

Sir William Blackstone.

THE LAWYER'S FAREWELL TO HIS MUSE.

I.

Companion of my tender age,
Serenely gay and sweetly sage,
How blithesome were we wont to rove
By verdant hill or shady grove,
Where fervent bees, with humming voice,
Around the honied oak rejoice,
And aged elms, with awful bend,
In long cathedral walks extend;
Lulled by the lapse of gliding floods,
Cheered by the warbling of the woods,
How blest my days, my thoughts how free,
In sweet society with thee!
Then all was joyous, all was young,
And years unheeded rolled along.

II.

But now the pleasing dream is o er,
These scenes must charm me now no more:
Lost to the fields and torn from you,
Farewell, a long, a last adieu.
Me wrangling courts and stubborn law,
To smoke, and crowds, and cities draw;

There selfish faction rules the day,
And pride and avarice throng the way;
Loose revelry and riot bold
In frighted streets their orgies hold;
Or, where in silence all is drowned,
Fell murder walks his nightly round.
No room for peace, no room for you,
Adieu, celestial nymph, adieu!

III.

Shakspeare, no more thy sylvan son,
Nor all the art of Addison,
Pope's heaven-strung lyre, nor Waller's ease,
Nor Milton's mighty self must please.
Instead of these, a formal band
With furs and coifs around me stand,
With sounds uncouth and accents dry
That grate the soul of harmony.
Each pedant sage unlocks his store
Of mystic, dark, discordant lore,
And points, with tottering hand, the ways
That lead me to the thorny maze.

IV.

Then, welcome business, welcome strife,
Welcome the cares, the thorns of life;
The visage wan, the pore-blind sight,
The toil by day, the lamp at night,
The tedious forms, the solemn prate,
The pert dispute, the dull debate,
The drowsy bench, the babbling hall;
For thee, fair Justice, welcome all.
Thus let my noon of life be past;
Yet, let my setting sun at last
Find out the still, the rural cell
Where sage retirement loves to dwell,
There let me taste the home-felt bliss
Of innocence and inward peace,

Untainted by the guilty bribe,
Uncursed amid the harpy tribe;
No orphan's cry to wound my ear,
My honour and my conscience clear.
Thus may I calmly meet my end,
Thus to the grave in peace descend!

OF the eminent lawyer who wrote the above verses I will subjoin a short memoir, for the gratification of those readers who will perhaps some day find themselves studying his renowned "Commentaries."

William Blackstone was born July 10th, 1723, in Cheapside. His father was a silk mercer,

"A citizen of credit and renown,"

himself the son of an eminent London apothecary. Of his four children William was the youngest. Sad to tell, he was a posthumous child: no fond father's welcome greeted his entrance into this fair world, and his mother, a delicate and gentle woman, after a few years of anxious widowhood, sank into an early grave before her youngest born had reached his twelfth year.

Happily the care of the boy's education was undertaken by his maternal uncle, Mr. Thomas Biggs, a surgeon of some reputation in the metropolis, and to whose affection his three orphan nephews were indebted for the liberal education which prepared them to work their way to respectability and competence, and, in the case of the youngest, to the acquirement of distinction and permanent renown.

I feel disposed here to digress for a moment, to observe what a blessing are family ties, the endearing bonds of consanguinity, and in how many happy ways their influence is exerted. Surely it is a peculiar and most delightful appellation given in Holy Scripture to the Almighty: "The God of the families of the whole earth," sealing, as it seems to do, with a special divine benediction, family love, work, and co-operation.

When about seven years old, little Willie was put to school at the Charter-House, and a few years later was admitted upon the foundation. It soon appeared that he was a diligent and industrious boy, and before long he became the favourite of his masters, who, perceiving that he would repay their care, encouraged him in his studies, and brought him forward as much as possible. Thus it came to pass that, by the time he was fifteen years old, he was the acknowledged head of the school, and, young as he was, was deemed well qualified for the university.

Accordingly, he was entered a commoner at Pembroke College, Oxford, and was elected to one of the Charter-House exhibitions, when an opportunity was afforded him of delivering the usual anniversary oration; upon which occasion he came off with flying colours, and shortly after obtained the gold prize medal for verses upon Milton. From boyhood he cherished a fondness for the Muses, and took delight in the study of our classical poets. Like many youths of a similar turn, he produced a variety of "juvenile poems," which he read for the entertainment of his chosen playmates and associates; yet he did not venture to publish these early effusions, although the friendly critics whom he consulted pronounced them worthy of so promising a genius.

In the meantime, he studied with unremitting diligence, and, prompted by his natural predilection, devoted much attention to the Greek and Roman poets, yet not neglecting logic, mathematics, and the other sciences. To one branch of mathematics he gave especial care—that of architecture, of which he was through life very fond. By such diligent application he gradually laid the foundation of future excellence. It does not appear how he was led to the choice of the law as his profession; evidently the "pleasing dreams" of his youth had turned to very different scenes from those presented by "wrangling courts and stubborn law;" but to these fond visions necessity compelled him to bid adieu, and on the 20th of November 1741, he entered himself of the Middle Temple, and prepared to betake himself seriously to the business of studying the "mystic, dark, discordant lore."

No wonder he heaved a sigh, and cast a lingering look behind. So has many a one done before and since; but, in the end, this labour has turned to profit. To be sure, he was only eighteen years old, and, in his case, it required no common self-denial and resolution to give his whole and undivided attention to the uncongenial task.

To succeed in the path he had chosen, he must be prudent, patient, and persevering. Doubtless he called to mind the classical adage—

> "Qui studet obstatam cursu contingere metam
> Multa tulit fecitque puer."

In the month of November 1743 Mr. Blackstone was elected member of All Souls' College, and, three years later, was called to the bar. After an experience of seven years in the courts at Westminster, it became evident that his talents were not adapted to forensic display. In fact, he was deficient in the more attractive qualifications of an orator. He had neither grace of delivery nor a lively flow of eloquence, and his manners were reserved and diffident. Owing, in a great measure, to his being very near-sighted, his brow was contracted, and the impression he made upon a casual observer was that of a somewhat stern and rigid man. In reality, he was benevolent, kind, and charitable; but, like many men who have to exercise constant self-discipline, he was impatient of the trifling and thoughtless habits of too many of those with whom he was associated.

In his college he was valued as he deserved to be, and his friendships there were warm and steady. Disheartened by want of success, as he advanced into mature life he determined to retire to his fellowship, intending to lead an academic life, and content himself with the occasional practice of his profession as a provincial counsel. It surely may afford some encouragement to struggling young lawyers to know, that the talents of such a man as Blackstone were, for a long time, so much overlooked, that his limited business failed even to cover his very moderate expenses, and, in order to support himself, he was compelled to depend upon his fellowship and on private lecturing.

Accordingly, in Michaelmas Term 1753, he commenced reading two lectures on the laws of England, to a numerous and interested audience. In a short time, so great was the attraction offered by these readings, together with the acknowledged abilities of the lecturer, that they came to be attended by crowded classes of young men of the first families and of the highest expectations. Among these auditors was one—a keen-witted lad of sixteen*—who afterwards became the

* Jeremy Bentham.

severest critic of his master's great work, the "Commentaries," and who pretended that, even at that early age, he listened with doubt and dissatisfaction to many of the axioms of the lecturer. Nevertheless, he has done ample justice to that which all unite in admiring—the beauty of Blackstone's style:—"Correct, elegant, unembarrassed, ornamented, it could scarcely fail to recommend itself to all readers. . . . In short, it is Blackstone who, first of all institutional writers, has taught jurisprudence to speak the language of the scholar and the gentleman; put a polish upon that rugged science; cleansed her from the dust and cobwebs of the office; and, if he has not enriched her with that precision which is drawn only from the sterling treasury of the sciences, has decked her out to advantage from the toilet of classical erudition, enlivened her with metaphors and allusions, and sent her abroad in some measure to instruct, and in still greater measure to entertain, the most miscellaneous and even the most fastidious societies. The merit to which, as much, perhaps, as to any, the work stands indebted for its reputation, is the enchanting harmony of its numbers."

After reading such a critique, we wonder not that the young Oxonians flocked to listen to the enchanter who could make the dullest theme so attractive. Almost the first publication of Blackstone was a useful manual entitled, "An Analysis of the Laws of England," designed to serve as a guide to the host of his students, and, at the same time, as an assistance to himself in performing the duties of his class-room. In 1758 he was unanimously elected first Vinerian professor, with a salary of £200. His introductory lecture was greatly admired, and was afterwards prefixed to the first volume of the Commentaries. By this time his fame had spread far and wide, and he was requested to read before the Prince of Wales; an honour which he declined, pleading that he did not think himself justified in breaking his engagements with his class at Oxford. So devoted, indeed, was he to the duties of his lectureship, that, it is said, during the many years he read his lectures at the university, no one could remember that he had ever kept his audience waiting for him even for a few minutes. "Melancthon himself," says his biographer, "could not have been more rigid in observing the hour and minute of an appointment."

The great Oxonian law-lecturer had now only to make his re-appearance in the legal courts of the metropolis to find himself at once in extensive practice, and to be offered the honours of his profession. Still, however, he continued to pass some part of the year at the university, and continued to read his lectures as before; while, in the autumn of 1759, he published a new edition of "The Great Charter, and the Charter of the Forest." This work added greatly to his reputation, not only as an accomplished lawyer, but as an accurate antiquary and an able historian.

Shortly after this time, a dissolution of Parliament having taken place, Mr. Blackstone was returned as one of the representatives of Hindon in Wiltshire, and had a patent of procedure granted him to rank as King's counsel, having declined the office of Chief-Justice of the Common Pleas in Ireland. His practice now being amply remunerative, he married, in the spring of 1761, Sarah, the daughter of James Clitherow, Esq., of Boston House, Middlesex. He was blessed with a large family of children, and enjoyed in domestic life the happiness for which his natural disposition especially fitted him. In the year 1765 appeared the first volume of the renowned "Commentaries on the Laws of England." The history of a work which has become so universal a text-book, and which has "almost rendered the abstruse science to which it is devoted a popular study," cannot be devoid of interest. The period at which the author first contemplated the composition of the "Commentaries" does not appear; but unquestionably he was led to the subject by the preparation of his private lectures at the university. It is, therefore, to these readings, and the studies connected with them, that the public is indebted for this *opus magnum.*

A very interesting passage in Halliday's Life of Lord Mansfield relates that, in the earlier part of Justice Blackstone's professional life, the chair of civil law at Oxford having become vacant, the Duke of Newcastle consulted Mr. Murray, the Solicitor-General (afterwards Lord Mansfield), on the selection of a proper person to fill the vacancy. The Solicitor-General warmly recommended Mr. Blackstone, who was accordingly introduced to the Duke. Being desirous of ascertaining the principles of the candidate, his Grace observed that, in case of any political agitation in the University, he might, he presumed, rely upon Mr. Blackstone's exertions in behalf of Government. "Your Grace may be assured that I will discharge my duty in giving law-lectures to the best of my poor ability," was the reply. "And your duty in the other branch, too?" added the Duke. Mr. Blackstone merely bowed in reply; and a few days afterwards Dr. Jenner was appointed to the vacant chair.

The reception which the "Commentaries" met with was most flattering. By Sir W. Jones they were pronounced "the most correct and beautiful outline that ever was exhibited of any human science;" and Lord Mansfield, shortly after their publication, being requested to point out the books proper for the perusal of a student, is said to have replied: "Until of late, I could never, with any satisfaction to myself, answer that question; but since the publication of Mr. Blackstone's 'Commentaries,' I can never be at a loss." On the other hand, the work did not escape the severity of criticism, and a host of censors arose to attack many of its positions with determined zeal and ability.

Although moderate in his political sentiments, Blackstone was a firm supporter of constitutional views, and was patronized by the Conservative Government of the day. In 1770 he was offered the situation of Solicitor-General, which he declined. He was then made one of the justices of the Court of Common Pleas. As he disliked the contentions of parties, one of the consequences of his elevation on which he most congratulated himself, was his removal from the House of Commons, "where," he used to remark, "amidst the rage of contending parties, a man of moderation must expect to meet no quarter from any side."

As a judge, he does not seem to have distinguished himself above his fellows, although, as might have been expected, his judgments were never deficient in learning and good sense. His talents for general business were very superior, and he discharged, with great advantage to the interests of the University, the various offices he had undertaken there.

He did not for any long time enjoy the honours and distinction to which his learning, his literature, and his diligence had raised him. His death occurred on the 14th February 1780, in the fifty-seventh year of his age.

The notes of decisions which Sir William had collected, both at the bar and while on the bench, were published after his death, pursuant to the directions of his will.

IX.

Lord Erskine.

"Nostræ eloquentiæ forensis facile princeps."

THE line placed at the head of the page is inscribed upon an admirable bust of Lord Erskine, by Nollekens; and, according to universal award, this great Nisi Prius leader bore the palm from all his compeers—nay, it is even doubted whether his eloquence was ever surpassed by ancient or modern forensic orator.

Lord Campbell, in his Lives of the Chancellors, has given a striking sketch of his truly surprising career. He has told how, on the 10th January, 1750, in a small, ill-furnished room, in an upper "flat" of a very lofty house in the Old Town of Edinburgh, was born the youngest son of Henry David, tenth Earl of Buchan, a peer of ancient pedigree, but now reduced to the verge of poverty, and burdened with a numerous family. The Honourable Thomas Erskine had two brothers older than himself, for whom it was necessary first to provide, and the means of his parents were exhausted before his turn came. There was nothing they could do but send him to sea as a midshipman; and though he had no liking for the profession, he was obliged to submit, and, when fourteen years old, entered the royal navy.

At the age of eighteen he lost his father, when, resolved not to return to sea, he decided to try his fortune in the army. Scarcely had he passed two years of military life, when he fell in love and married. Shortly after this event his regiment was ordered to Minorca, and there, for two years, he was stationed. Shut up in this small island, far removed from congenial society, and thrown upon his own resources, he applied himself diligently to study, and to the cultivation of the naturally powerful genius with which he was endowed. Laboriously and systematically he went through a course of English literature, and familiarized himself with the immortal classics of our language. Shakspeare and Milton, Dryden and Pope were read and re-read, until he had them almost by heart.

At length, in the spring of 1772, he returned to England; and we catch the first glimpse of him in the pages of Boswell, who relates that, dining with Dr. Johnson at Sir A. Macdonald's, he met a young officer in the regimentals of the Scots Royals, "who talked with vivacity, fluency, and precision so uncommon, that he attracted particular attention. On inquiry, he proved to be the Honourable Thomas Erskine, who afterwards attained such brilliant reputation at the bar in Westminster." The prospects of the young ensign at this time were dismal in the extreme; he had no money to purchase a higher commission, and the irksomeness of his situation was increased by his having to keep his wife and family in a barrack-room or in lodgings, while he moved about with his regiment from place to place.

Conscious of the great powers he possessed, he felt that he was fitted for better things than the wretched existence which seemed to await him—to be spent in listlessness and penury.

At this juncture of his history it so chanced that, in a town in which he was quartered, the assizes were held, and the lounging lieutenant—*faute de mieux*—strolled into the court to pass an idle hour. His appearance attracted the attention of Lord Mansfield, the presiding judge, who inquired concerning him, and upon learning that he was the younger brother of the Earl of Buchan, who had sailed with his nephew, invited him to sit on the bench by his side, explained to him the nature of the proceedings that were going forward, and showed him the utmost civility.

"Erskine heard a cause of considerable interest tried, in which the counsel were supposed to display great eloquence. Never undervaluing his own powers, he thought within himself that he could have made a better speech than any of them, on whichever side he had been retained. The thought then suddenly struck him that it might not even now be too late for him to study the law and be called to the bar. Lord Mansfield invited him to dinner, and being greatly struck with his conversation and pleased with his manners, detained him till late in the evening. When the rest of the company had withdrawn, the lieutenant, who ever showed great moral courage, in consideration of the connection between the Murrays and the Erskines, and the venerable Earl's great kindness and condescension, disclosed to him his plan of a change of profession, with a modest statement of his reasons. Lord Mansfield by no means discouraged him, but advised him, before he took a step so serious, to consult his near relations."

Such was the "accident" that gave the turn to all his future history, and led to his attaining the highest honours of the profession he embraced. With the consent of his family he immediately entered himself at Lincoln's Inn, and matriculated at Cambridge, being entered on the books of Trinity College as a gentleman commoner. While a law student, during the three years which followed his retirement from the army, notwithstanding the assistance of friends, he was in great pecuniary straits. Although exercising the strictest economy and the most rigid self-denial, he found it a difficult matter to provide for the necessities of every day, and was pronounced by Jeremy Bentham to be "so shabbily dressed as was quite remarkable." Another of his associates gives the following lively description of him at this juncture: "The young student resided in small lodgings near Hampstead, and openly avowed that he lived on cow-beef, because he could not afford any of a superior quality, dressed shabbily, expressed the greatest gratitude to Mr. Harris for occasional free admissions to Covent Garden, and used boastingly to exclaim to my father, 'Thank fortune, out of my own family, I don't know a lord!'"

The time, however, arrived when all this was to be changed, and a sudden and surprising transition from want to abundance, and from obscurity to splendour awaited him. So speedy a rise is unexampled, save in the fairy tales of the Arabian Nights. On the 3d day of July, 1778, he was called to the bar, and on the 24th November, in Michaelmas Term, he made his first appearance before the public. It was the critical day in his life, and exhibited the most remarkable scene ever witnessed in Westminster Hall. His prospects seemed dark enough, for he was unknown and had no connections to assist him, nor were any of the attorneys acquainted with his merits. But he had one retainer, which came to him in a singular manner and most unexpectedly. There was a certain Captain Baillie, a veteran seaman of great worth, who, for his services, held an office at the Greenwich Hospital, in which establishment he discovered the grossest abuses. After vainly endeavouring by remonstrance to procure a redress of these evils, he published a statement of the case, relating simply the actual facts, and reflecting with just severity upon Lord Sandwich, First Lord of the Admiralty, who, for electioneering purposes, had placed in the Hospital a great number of landsmen. Captain Baillie was immediately suspended by the Board of Admiralty, and some of the inferior agents, instigated by Lord Sandwich, who himself hung back, filed a criminal information for libel against him. The case excited great public interest, and the circumstances were everywhere canvassed. During the Long Vacation Erskine had met Captain Baillie (to whom he was personally unknown) at a friend's house, and, after dinner, expressed himself warmly on the corrupt and scandalous practices imputed to Lord Sandwich in the matter. Inquiring who the young man was, Baillie was informed that he had just been called to the bar, and had formerly been in the navy; when he immediately said, "Then, I'll have him for my counsel." They parted without having been introduced to each other, but the Captain did not forget his purpose, and the next day, as the young advocate sat briefless and desponding in his chambers, a slip of paper was brought to him with the words written upon it:—

"King's Bench. The King *v.* Baillie.
Retainer for the Defendant, the Honourable Thomas Erskine,
one guinea;"

and a yellow golden guinea, his first fee (which he long preserved as a curiosity), was put into his hand.

When Michaelmas Term came round, a brief was delivered him; but to his dismay he found upon it the names of four senior counsel, and, despairing of being heard after so many predecessors, he gave himself no trouble to prepare for the occasion. Yet fortune favoured him. When the cause came on, the affidavits were so long, and the four senior counsel so tedious, that it was almost dark when the last argument was brought to a conclusion. Lord Mansfield therefore adjourned the case till the next morning, and thus was time given to the young advocate to prepare his thoughts and nerve himself for his first speech at the bar. On the following day, the judges having taken their seats, and the court being crowded with an eager audience, to the general surprise, "there arose from the back row a young gentleman, whose name as well as whose face was unknown to almost all present, and who, in a collected, firm, but sweet, modest, and conciliating tone" commenced his address. After a short exordium, he proceeded to show that his client had written nothing but the truth, and had acted strictly within the line of his duty. He then denounced, in vehement and indignant language, the injustice which had suspended such a man from his office without proof of his guilt, and mentioned Lord Sandwich by name; when Lord Mansfield interfered, reminding the counsel that the First Lord of the Admiralty was not before the Court.

Erskine. "I know that he is not formally before the Court, but, for that very reason, *I will bring him before the Court.* He has placed these men in the front of the battle, in hopes to escape under their shelter, but I will not join in battle with them; their vices, though screwed up to the highest pitch of human depravity, are not of dignity enough to vindicate the combat with *me.* I will drag *him* to light who is the dark mover behind this scene of iniquity. I assert that the Earl of Sandwich has but one road to escape out of this business without pollution and disgrace—and that is by publicly disavowing the acts of the prosecutors, and restoring Captain Baillie to his command. . . . . If, on the contrary, he continues to protect the prosecutors in spite of the evidence of their guilt, which has excited the abhorrence of the numerous audience who crowd this Court, *if he keep this injured man suspended, or dares to turn that suspension into a removal, I shall then not scruple to declare him an accomplice in their guilt, a shameless oppressor, a disgrace to his rank, and a traitor to his trust.*

"My lords, this matter is of the last importance. I speak not as an *advocate* alone—I speak to you as a *man*—as a member of a state whose very existence depends upon her naval strength. If our fleets are to be crippled by the baneful influence of elections, *we are lost indeed.* If the seaman, while he exposes his body to fatigues and dangers, looking forward to Greenwich as an asylum for infirmity and old age, sees the gates of it blocked up by corruption, and hears the riot and mirth of luxurious landsmen drowning the groans and complaints of the wounded helpless companions of his glory—he will tempt the seas no more. The Admiralty may press *his body* indeed, at the expense of humanity and the constitution, but they cannot press *his mind;* they cannot press the heroic ardour of a British sailor; and instead of a fleet to carry terror all round the globe, the Admiralty may not be able much longer to amuse us with even the peaceable unsubstantial pageant of a review. (There had just before been a naval review at Portsmouth.)

"*Fine and imprisonment!* The man deserves a *palace* instead of a *prison* who prevents the palace built by the public bounty of his country from being converted into a dungeon, and who sacrifices his own security to the interests of humanity and virtue!"

The impression made by this address is said to have been unprecedented. Lord Campbell thus remarks upon it,—"I must own, that, all the circumstances considered, it is the most wonderful forensic effort of which we have any account in our annals. It was the *début* of a barrister just called and wholly unpractised in public speaking, before a court crowded with the men of the greatest distinction, belonging to all parties in the state. He came after four eminent counsel, who might have been supposed to have exhausted the subject. He was called to order by a venerable judge whose word had been law in that hall above a quarter of a century. His exclamation, 'I will bring him before the court!' and the crushing denunciation of Lord Sandwich, in which he was enabled to persevere, from the sympathy of the bystanders and even of the judges, who, in strictness, ought to have checked his irregularity—are as soul-stirring as anything in this species of eloquence presented to us by ancient or modern times."

Such was the first effort of this extraordinary man—a brilliant commencement to an unexampled career of success and honour. What must have been the emotions that he experienced when he received the congratulations of all around him, and knew that his anxieties were at an end—that he had won fame for himself and independence and comfort for those he loved? "I succeeded," he afterwards said, "quite to my own satisfaction, (sometimes the surest proof that you have satisfied others,) and, as I marched along the hall, after the rising of the judges, the attorneys flocked around me with their briefs." He was asked how he had the courage to stand up so boldly against Lord Mansfield, when he made this charming answer, that he thought his little children were plucking his robe, and that he heard them saying, "Now, father, is the time to get us bread!"

He was at once in full business. Briefs and fees—large and small—flowed in a continual stream into the chambers of the counsellor who had so astonished the world. It is said that when, shortly after, he joined the Home Circuit—where his fame had preceded him, and he was immediately in full employment—he astonished one of his companions by a prophecy of his future honours. Riding over an extensive heath between Lewes and Guildford with William Adam, afterwards Lord Chief Commisioner of the Jury Court in Scotland, he suddenly exclaimed, "Willie! the time will come when I shall wear the robes of Lord Chancellor, and the star of the thistle will blaze on my breast!"

The name of Lord Erskine recalls vividly to my mind the recollection of my honoured friend, Mrs. Opie. Shortly before her marriage she was present at the famous trials of Horne Tooke, Holcroft, and others, for treason, at the Old Bailey, in the year 1794, when Lord Erskine won his greatest triumphs in the defence of the liberties of his countrymen and the independence of the press. That was indeed a day of alarm, and the whole nation trembled in a state of excitement almost inconceivable at the present day. The venerable city of Norwich, in which Miss Alderson resided, had rather an evil reputation; for it was suspected that not a few turbulent spirits there were in correspondence with the parent societies, whose professed object was parliamentary reform, and whose proceedings were often very objectionable and unwise.

The greatest apprehension was felt on the part of the government; the whole land swarmed with spies and informers; and at length ministers adopted the almost incredible course of a prosecution for high treason. It may be imagined with what intense interest these proceedings were regarded by a young and ardent woman, who sympathized warmly with those whom she had been taught to think "patriots." She had, besides, personally, much at stake, for upon the issue of these trials depended her future lot in life. Had the prosecution been successful, Dr. Alderson and many of his friends and associates had determined to quit England and emigrate to America. Under these circumstances she hailed with eager satisfaction the opportunity of accompanying a friend to the Old Bailey, and in her letters home gave a lively account of the events which transpired. It is a curious proof of the terrorism which prevailed that it was judged prudent to destroy these letters, written in confidence by a young lady to her domestic circle!*

Many years subsequently, when recalling the events of that period, Mrs. Opie related an anecdote with reference to these trials, in which Lord Erskine played the principal part. The incident took place in the year 1813, when Madame de Staël was residing for some months in London, having been exiled by Napoleon from France. One morning Mrs. Opie, who had formed the acquaintance of the illustrious stranger, called on her by appointment, accompanied by a friend whom she desired to see on some particular business. Scarcely had that business been concluded when the servant announced Lord Erskine, who came in with a book in his hands, and, as soon as he perceived Mrs. Opie, exclaimed, "I am rejoiced to see you here, for I want you to read something for me." He then bowed gracefully to Madame de Staël and presented her two books, which, he said, contained his most celebrated speeches, and opening the

I remember to have heard of a curious scene enacted in one of the dissenting chapels of Norwich on the occasion. The well-known Mark Wilks was in the pulpit, conducting the service on Sunday morning. One of his congregation was expected home from London, having been eagerly watching the trials, which terminated on the day previous. His return was awaited with intense interest; for in those days there were no magical wires to carry tidings with lightning-speed. The slow-moving stage-coach performed its tedious journey, and was, that eventful morning, "over time." The hour for worship had arrived, and the congregation had entered upon the solemn duties, but, every now and then, an involuntary glance in the direction of the entrance told that attention was distracted. At length the door opened, and the well-known figure of the expected traveller was seen advancing up the aisle. Mr. Wilks immediately paused, and looking towards him exclaimed, "How is it, brother?" "All is well," was the reply. "Then," said the minister, in a voice of deep emotion, "let us sing, 'Praise God from whom all blessings flow.'" This invitation was responded to by the simultaneous rising of the assembly who joined heart and soul in the anthem.

first volume, he turned to the blank page, on which he had written a dedication to La Baronne de Staël in English, which he begged Mrs. Opie to read to her. But the lady, eagerly taking the book, said, "I can read it myself." Accordingly she began, though with very poor success, the writing being probably difficult for a foreigner to decipher; and the unfortunate author had to endure the misery of hearing his smooth and elegant sentences deprived of their charm, by being stammered out, and possibly not perfectly understood.

It must have been no small trial to the nerves of a man so sensitive and so vain as was Lord Erskine, but he endured it with politeness, and quickly recovered his equanimity. Then taking the second volume, which contained his speeches at the Old Bailey trials, he read her some favourite passages; and finished by alluding to the evident dislike which the Lord Chief Baron Eyre, who presided at them, entertained for him, and how strongly he proved it during the trial of Horne Tooke:—

"He then," says Mrs. Opie, "related what had passed between himself and the Chief-Justice after the trial was over and the crowd dispersed, and which I, who was present, well remembered, having, by accident, overheard. Liking to be near the eloquent man, and to hear him speak, I had contrived to get so near as to overhear what passed, and which I thought was too loud not to be intended to be heard. The judge had, I saw, to repeat what he said; but at length he was answered in a manner which he little expected, for the indignant speaker replied, 'My lord, I am willing to give your lordship such an answer as an aggrieved man of honour like myself is willing to give to the man who has repeatedly insulted him, and I am willing and ready to meet your lordship at any time and place which you may choose to appoint.' At this point of the story Madame de Staël cried, 'What, my lord? that was a challenge *n'est ce pas?*' 'Yes, ma'am.'—'Well, what did he say?' 'Oh, nothing to the purpose, but I assure you that I was irritated into saying what I did.'—'Yes, indeed. I was behind you, Lord Erskine (said I), and heard all that passed; and though such things were quite new to me, I felt sure what was said by you amounted to a challenge; but when I told your friends with whom I went home what had passed, they said I was a silly girl, and that I was mistaken.' He looked at me with some surprise, and, I fear, with a doubt of my veracity. Probably he thought I was romancing. Certainly it was a curious fact or coincidence, that this conversation, overheard by me in the year 1794, I should be present to hear related by Lord Erskine himself in the year 1813. The circumstance and the words he has published at the end of the trial of Horne Tooke."

On another occasion she thus describes the impression his appearance made upon her at first sight,—"Well do I remember him, as I first saw him, entering for a few minutes and taking a hasty survey of the court. I was immediately struck with the look of intelligent inquiry which he cast over the eager crowd assembled to hear him; that eye reminded me of the description of Ledyard, the eastern traveller's eye, for it seemed 'bright and restless;' and its rapid glance appeared to observe, in its brief survey, as much as other eyes in a more lengthened one." Not long after this they became personally acquainted with each other at the house of a mutual friend near London, when, in the course of conversation, Lord Erskine mentioned that he was going down special to Huntingdon on a most interesting occasion. A young man, lately come into possession of a large fortune, had been proceeded against by the next heir as being a supposititious child; and he said that he was counsel for the defence, and added that the cause was likely to be very long and very interesting, as the defendant was universally beloved. He finished by promising that on his return he would call and give his friends an account of the trial.

Mrs. Opie, with characteristic vivacity, describes the next meeting,—"Great was my impatience till the appointed day came, and the great orator arrived. But though he talked most pleasantly, and on law subjects too, not one single allusion did he make to the Huntingdon case. In vain did I try to take courage and remind him of his promise. I was not then a married woman, and fancied it would be presuming to do so; but when I heard his carriage announced, and saw him about to depart, made valiant by despair, I exclaimed, 'Oh, Mr. Erskine, you have not fulfilled your promise! You have not told us the particulars of the Huntingdon cause. 'True,' he replied, starting and turning back, 'but you shall not be disappointed;' and leading me to the sofa, he seated himself beside me, and went through the whole of the proceedings. He gave us the evidence on both sides, told us what his opponent had said for the plaintiff, and he for the defendant; and, warming as he proceeded, he soon grew as much interested in the proceedings as we were; and when he came to the verdict of the jury, which was in favour of his client, his countenance beamed with animation while he described the general plaudit with which the verdict was received in the court, and the shouts which were heard outside the walls from the assembled multitude. He then hastily jumped into his carriage, leaving me exulting in having drawn from him a gratification so unusual and so complete."

The greatest treat was still in store for this enthusiastic admirer. It was in the year 1805 that she again heard Mr. Erskine, when he made a brilliant speech at the Norwich assizes, in a Right of Way case. Through life Mrs. Opie was in the habit of attending the assize court, and she was usually among the very earliest personages who entered its precincts, eagerly awaiting the commencement of proceedings. Of this propensity, the following note, which she once addressed to me, is an amusing evidence:—

"My Cecilia Lucy,—The judges always, as I believe, go to church first, and take the sacrament afterwards. But I *always* go early to be sure of a good seat; so I mean to call thee at nine; and we can talk there as well as here—and the time will soon fly. I went in a chariot fly to see them come in. Farewell! little dear; I fear thou art a lazy-bones, but indeed, by ten I have often seen the best places filled. Often, how often, both as a young and old woman, have I been in that court by half-past seven in the morning—was, this time twelve-month. A. O."

Urged by the desire to hear the Prince of Pleaders, she was very early in court to obtain a seat by the side of the judge, Sir Alexander Macdonald, and saw and heard everything to the greatest advantage. There she remained the whole day, excepting a short time when she retired to take tea, but soon returned to her post and stayed all night unwilling to leave lest she should miss hearing the great orator. As hour after hour passed by, and witness succeeded witness, the audience became gradually smaller, some even of the jury began to nod for very weariness, and it seemed likely that, except the judge, the high sheriff, the barristers, the officers of the court, and *herself*, there would soon be no hearers left awake, and the beams of the rising day were beginning to show themselves through the windows!

"The observant Erskine took the hint, so palpably given, and coming up to me kindly said, 'Go home, go home! I shall not reply to-night, but you had better be here by eight in the morning;' and soon after the court adjourned to that hour..... I was in court again by half-past seven, but too late to obtain a seat, and I stood many hours in a painful position, but I was soon made unconscious of it by the eloquence of Erskine; for during those hours he spoke, and hushed a court, crowded even to suffocation, into the most perfect stillness. Never was the power of an orator over his audience more evident or more complete.

"The plaintiff gained the cause, and her advocate new laurels; for I know that those best qualified to form a correct judgment on the subject, namely, his brother lawyers who were present, declared that they had 'never before heard Mr. Erskine so great in reply.' Fortunate, therefore, were those who heard him that day, as never again was he heard to equal advantage. A few months afterwards he was made Lord Chancellor, and when, while talking to him at a party in London, I told him I was every day intending to go into the Court of Chancery in hope of hearing him speak in his new capacity, his reply was, 'Pray, do not come, you will not hear anything worth the trouble. I am nothing now; you heard the last and best of me at Norwich last year!'

"This was indeed too true, and those powers of forensic eloquence for which he was so celebrated were not necessary on the judgment seat or in the court of chancery, and would have been in a measure thrown away in the House of Lords. Fortunate, therefore, I repeat it, were those who heard him in the Right of Way cause in Norwich; and when he forcibly reminded me of the portrait of Garrick, so admirably drawn by the pen of Sheridan in his unequalled monody—a portrait which might have been supposed to be that of the Honourable Thomas Erskine, for his indeed were—

'The grace of action, the adapted mien,
Faithful as nature to the varied scene;
The expressive glance, whose subtle comment draws
Entranced attention, and a mute applause:
Gesture that marks, with sense of feeling fraught,
A sense in silence, and a will in thought.
Harmonious speech, whose pure and liquid tone
Gives verse a music scarce confessed its own:
As light from gems assumes a brighter ray,
And clothed with orient hues transcends the day.
Passion's wild break, and frowns that awe the sense,
And every charm of gentler eloquence.'"

It seems by common consent agreed that the finest of all Lord Erskine's orations is his speech in the defence of Stockdale, "whose trial may be termed the Case of Libels." It is justly regarded by all English lawyers as a consummate specimen of the art of addressing a jury, and is besides a model of all that constitutes the poetry of eloquence. Lord Abinger, who was present in court when this speech was delivered, told his son-in-law, Lord Campbell, that the effect upon the audience was wholly unexampled. They were, so to speak, electrified by the marvellous power of sympathy which the accomplished orator knew so perfectly how to awaken and to sustain.

It is, I think, very interesting to learn that Lord Erskine himself set a pre-eminent value on his speech in the prosecution of Paine for his blasphemous publication, "The Age of Reason." This speech is, indeed, a noble apology for Christianity, and appears to have been the utterance of his sincere conviction. "The people of England," he said emphatically, "are a religious people, and with the blessing of God, so far as it is in my power, I will lend my aid to keep them so." In his opening address to the jury, he said, "For my own part, gentlemen, I have ever been deeply devoted to the truths of Christianity, and my firm belief in the holy gospel is by no means owing to the prejudices of education, but has arisen from the fullest and most continued reflections of my riper years and understanding. It forms at this moment the great consolation of a life which as a shadow passes away; and without it I should consider my long course of health and prosperity (too long, perhaps, and too uninterrupted to be good for any man) only as the dust which the wind scatters, and rather as a snare than a blessing." Then, having adverted to some of the most obnoxious parts of the book, he burst into a glowing apostrophe of the devout, holy, and sublime spirits who have, in all ages, held to the faith of God's word, and appealed to the testimony of Milton, Boyle, Locke, and

Hale, finishing with Milton, the illustrious one, who, having been deprived of the natural light of the body, enjoyed the clear shining of the celestial day, which enabled him to "justify the ways of God to man!"

Before concluding, he uttered the following passage, full of simple pathos and beauty:—"I can conceive a distressed but virtuous man, surrounded by his children, looking up to him for bread, when he has none to give them, sinking under his last day's labour, and unequal to the next, yet still supported by confidence in the hour when all tears shall be wiped from the eyes of affliction, bearing the burden laid upon him by a mysterious Providence which he adores, and anticipating with exultation the revealed promises of his Creator, when he shall be greater than the greatest, and happier than the happiest of mankind."

In a letter he afterwards wrote with reference to this prosecution, he says,—"My opening speech, correctly as it was uttered in court, is in Mr. Ridgway's collection of my speeches at the bar. It was first printed by the Society for the Suppression of Vice, and circulated to a very wide extent, which gave me the greatest satisfaction, as I would rather that all my other speeches were committed to the flames, or in any manner buried in oblivion, than that a single page of it should be lost."

One naturally asks, What were the characteristics of this great man's eloquence, which made it so surpassingly impressive? We are told by Lord Campbell that he was not indebted for his success to the richness of ornament or of illustration, to wit, to humour, or to sarcasm. His first great excellence was his devotion to his client; he utterly forgot himself in the character he represented. From the moment the jury were sworn he thought of nothing but the verdict, till it was recorded in his favour. Earnestness and energy were ever present throughout his speeches, impressing his argument on the mind of his hearer with a force which seemed to compel conviction. Another marked peculiarity was the familiar knowledge he displayed of the secret workings of the human mind. "He spoke as his clients would respectively have spoken, being endowed with his genius." There must also be taken into account "the exquisite sweetness of his diction, pure, simple, and mellifluous—the cadences not being borrowed from any model, nor following any rule, but marked by constant harmony and variety." Nor did he neglect attention to those trifling matters which might add to the effect of his eloquence. He was always careful to be well dressed, and when he went into the country on special retainers, it was his custom to examine the court beforehand, that he might select the most advantageous place for addressing the jury.

But what his biographer especially notes and regards as more useful to hold up for imitation is his admirable demeanour, while engaged in business at the Bar, "to which, perhaps, his success was not less due than to his talents."

"Respectful to the judges, though ever ready to assert his independence,—courteous to the jury, while he boldly reminded them of their duties, free from asperity towards his opponents, constantly kind and considerate to his juniors, treating the witnesses as persons, generally speaking, reluctantly attending to assist in the investigation of truth, ... looking benevolently even on the *circum-*

stantes, and glad when he could accommodate them with a seat, of a gay and happy temperament, enjoying uninterruptedly a boyish flow of animal spirits, and enlivening the dullest cause with his hilarity and good humour, he was a universal favourite; there was a general desire, as far as law and justice would permit, that he should succeed, and the *prestige* of his reputation was considered the sure forerunner of victory."

In his later years Lord Erskine withdrew entirely from public life. His friends and admirers delighted to enjoy his society and to visit him at his beautiful villa at Hampstead, called "Evergreen Hall." Here he gave gay parties, of which he was the life, by his mirth, *bon-hommie*, and eccentricities. A lively description of one of these is given by Sir Sam. Romilly:—"I dined to-day at Lord Erskine's. Among the light and trifling topics of conversation after dinner it may be worth while to mention one, as it strongly characterizes him. He has always expressed and felt a great sympathy for animals. He has talked for years of a bill he was to bring into Parliament to prevent cruelty towards them. He has always had several favourite animals to whom he has been much attached, and of whom all his acquaintance have a number of anecdotes to relate:—A favourite dog which he used to bring, when he was at the Bar, to all his consultations—another favourite dog, which, at the time when he was Lord Chancellor, he himself rescued in the street from some boys who were about to kill it under pretence of its being mad—a favourite goose which followed him wherever he walked about his grounds—a favourite macaw—and other dumb favourites without number. He told us now that he had got two favourite leeches. He had been blooded by them last autumn when he had been taken dangerously ill at Portsmouth; they had saved his life, and he had brought them with him to town—had ever since kept them in a glass—had himself every day given them fresh water, and had formed a friendship with them. He said he was sure they both knew him and were grateful to him. He had given them different names, Home and Cline (the names of two celebrated surgeons), their dispositions being quite different. After a good deal of conversation about them, he went himself, brought them out of his library, and placed them in their glass upon the table. It is impossible, however, without the vivacity, the tones, the details, and the gestures of Lord Erskine, to give an adequate idea of this singular scene."

Many diverting stories are related of his "Sayings and Doings." After he had resigned the Chancellorship he used to amuse himself with horticultural pursuits. Sometimes he would take a spade in his hand and pretend to dig in his kitchen garden. On such occasions he would say, "Here I am enjoying my 'otium, cum diggin a taity!'" The garden was under the care of a Scotch gardener, who once coming to complain to him, as of a grievance to be remedied, that the drought had burnt up all the vegetables and was killing the shrubs; he said to him, "Well, John, all that I can do for you is to order the hay to be cut down to-morrow morning; and if that does not bring rain, nothing will!"

With a view to improve his property (an estate in Sussex), he began to study farming, and put himself under the celebrated Mr. Coke, of Norfolk, afterwards Earl of Leicester, observing that "having been instructed by *Coke* at Westminster, he was now to be instructed by *Coke* of Holkham, as great a man in his way." But the master found him a very unapt pupil, and used to relate that "coming to a finely cultivated piece of wheat, the first specimen he had seen of drill husbandry, Erskine exclaimed in a delighted tone, 'What a beautiful piece of *lavender!*'"

Not long after his resignation of the great Seal, he was invited to a fête at Oatlands, where the Duchess of York had upon the lawn a number of rare animals, and among others a black monkey with a long white hairy mantle flowing gracefully over his head and shoulders. Erskine was late in making his appearance; but at length, while a group of distinguished guests were standing near the entrance to the court yard, he drove up. Immediately alighting, instead of paying his respects to these gentlemen, he suddenly stepped up to the monkey, and in a very formal manner, making a profound congée to the animal, amid the laughter of the by-standers, thus addressed it:—"Sir, I sincerely wish you joy. You wear your wig for life!"

Of his jokes, consisting chiefly of puns, many were long remembered. Polito, the keeper of the wild beasts in Exeter Change, having brought an action against the proprietors of a stage-coach for negligence, whereby his portmanteau was stolen from the boot of the vehicle, he himself having been riding on the box, "Why did he not," said the defendant's witty counsel, "take a lesson from his own sagacious elephant and travel with his *trunk before him?*"

When he was Chancellor, being asked by the Secretary to the Treasury, whether he would attend the grand ministerial fish-dinner to be given at Greenwich, at the end of the session, he answered, "To be sure, I will; what would your fish-dinner be without the Great Seal?"

He could not resist a witticism though at the expense of a friend. His acquaintance, Mr. Maylem of Ramsgate, having mentioned that his physician had ordered him not to bathe,—"Oh, then," said Erskine, "you are *Malum prohibitum.*" "My wife, however," resumed the other, "does bathe." "That's worse still," was the retort, "for she is *Malum in se.*"

Occasionally in his exuberant fun he indulged in what may be called a practical joke. A worthy gentleman having proposed that a public testimonial should be presented to himself for his eminent services—in answer to one of his circulars, Erskine wrote on the first page of a letter in a flowing hand these words, which filled it to the bottom:—

"My Dear Sir John,—I am certain there are few in this kingdom who set a higher value on your public services than myself—and I have the honour to subscribe—"

Then, on turning over the leaf was to be found,—

"Myself,

"Your most obedient, faithful servant,

T. ERSKINE.

I will conclude this chapter with what appears to me an admirable vindication of the office of an ADVOCATE, by Lord Campbell:—

"Let us imagine to ourselves an advocate inspired by

a generous love of fame, and desirous of honourably assisting in the administration of justice, by obtaining redress for the injured and defending the innocent,—who has liberally studied the science of jurisprudence, and has stored his mind, and refined his taste, by a general acquaintance with elegant literature,—who has an intuitive insight into human character and the workings of human passion,—who possesses discretion as well as courage, and caution along with enthusiasm,—who is not only able, by his powers of persuasion, to give the best chance of success to every client whom he represents in every variety of private causes, but who is able to defeat conspiracies against public liberty, to be carried into effect by a perversion of the criminal law,—and who, by the victories which he gains, and the principles which he establishes, places the free constitution of his country on an imperishable basis! Such an advocate, in my opinion, stands quite as high in the scale of true greatness as the parliamentary leader, who ably opens a budget, who lucidly explains a new system of commercial policy, or who dexterously attacks the measures of the Government.

"I boldly affirm that there is no department of human intellect in which the *mens divinior* may be more refulgently displayed."

X.

Lord Ellenborough.

"Ellenborough was a real chief,—such as the rising generation of lawyers may read of and figure to themselves in imagination, but may never behold to dread or to admire."

THUS does Lord Campbell begin his delightful memoir of Lord Ellenborough; and he adds: "He was a man of gigantic intellect; he had the advantage of the very best education which England could bestow; he was not only a consummate master of his own profession, but well initiated in mathematical science, and one of the best classical scholars of his day. . . . . When I first entered Westminster Hall in my wig and gown I there found him 'monarch of all he surveyed,' and, at this distance of time, I can hardly recollect without awe his appearance and his manners as he ruled over his submissive subjects."

The early history of so remarkable a man cannot be without interest, and we trace with pleasure his upward progress. As the younger son of an English prelate of very great learning and very little wealth, his lot in life was highly favourable to his gaining distinction in the world,—affording him the best facilities and the strongest incentives for exertion. His father was Dr. Edmund Law, Bishop of Carlisle, who had distinguished himself in early life at St. John's College, Cambridge, and afterwards became noted in the literary world for his varied acquirements and numerous theological works, the most famous of which was a treatise "On the Intermediate State." He was married to Mary, daughter of John Christian, Esq., and they had a family of twelve children, among whom were two bishops and a Chief-Justice.

Edward, the last mentioned, was one of the youngest of this numerous race, and was born in the parsonage of Salkeld, on the 16th November, 1750. Resembling his mother much in features, he is said to have derived from her likewise his manners and the characteristic qualities of his mind; and when he had reached old age he often expressed a fond respect for her memory. The good bishop is thus described by his friend, Archdeacon Paley:—"His lordship was a man of great softness of manners, and of the mildest and most tranquil disposition. His voice was never raised above its ordinary pitch. His countenance seemed never to have been ruffled; it invariably preserved the same kind and composed aspect, truly indicating the calmness and benignity of his temper. His fault was too great a degree of inaction and facility in his public station. The bashfulness of his nature, with an extreme unwillingness to give pain, rendered him sometimes less firm and efficient in the administration of authority than was requisite."

It is difficult to imagine a character less resembling that of the sarcastic Chief-Justice, who certainly did not "take after" his amiable father.

The boy, though very troublesome, was a great favourite at home, where he remained till he was eight years old, when he was sent into Norfolk to live with his maternal uncle, the Rev. H. Christian, a clergyman settled at Dorking in that county. Having been for a short time at a school in Bury St. Edmunds, he was removed to the foundation of the Charter House in London. To his solid acquisitions there, he ever gratefully ascribed his subsequent eminence in public life; and there, by the special direction of his will, his remains were deposited, near those of the founder.

For six years Law continued at the Charter House, and rose to be captain of the school. He used to say that while enjoying this dignity he felt himself a much more important personage than when he rose to be Chief-Justice of England and a Cabinet minister. It is said that at this early period he showed the same vigour of character, and the same mixture of arrogance and *bon-hommie* which afterwards distinguished him. He was described by a class-fellow as a bluff, burly boy, at once moody and good-natured—ever ready to inflict a blow or perform an exercise for a school-fellow.

At the age of eighteen he was sent to Cambridge, and entered at Peterhouse, of which his father was Master. There he worked hard, and his straightforward manly character, joined to his brilliant talents, procured him, while at the University, friends as well as admirers. One of these was William Coxe, afterwards Archdeacon, who described the future Chief-Justice, in flattering terms:—"Of a warm and generous disposition, he breathes all the animation of youth and the spirit of freedom. His thoughts and conceptions are uncommonly great and striking; his language and his expressions are strong and nervous, and partake of his sentiments. As all his views are honest and his intentions direct, he scorns to disguise his feelings or palliate his sentiments. This disposition leads him to use a warmth of expression which sometimes assumes the appearance of *fierté* and has frequently disgusted his acquaintance. But his friends know the goodness of his heart and pardon a foible that arises from the candour and openness of his temper. Indeed, he never fails, when the heat of conversation is over, and when his mind becomes cool and dispassionate, to acknowledge the error of his nature, and, like a Roman Catholic, claim an absolution for past as well as future transgressions."

It would have been better had the youth, instead of simply acknowledging his fault, determined to conquer it. In the end it mastered him, and was a sad blot upon his character. That he exercised self-government in other things is evident, for, though he delighted in conviviality, he never wasted his time in idle amusements, but owned "the greatest struggle he ever made was in leaving a party and retiring to his rooms to read."

When the time came for taking his bachelor's degree, it was confidently expected that he would be senior wrangler and first medallist; but in this he was disappointed, being surpassed in the mathematical examinations by two men much inferior to him in talent, but of more steady application. He was deeply mortified, and though his classical acquirements carried the first medal, his pride was by no means assuaged, and he continued for the rest of his days to scoff at academical honours.

It was the earnest wish of Dr. Law to have all his sons in the Church; but Edward was bent upon trying his fortune at the bar, and by embracing the profession of the law *against* the strong desire of a father he sincerely respected and loved incurred a heavy responsibility. He had therefore the most powerful motives for exertion that he might justify his own opinion and soothe the feelings of a fond parent. Resolved to make his way he started on his career with a dogged determination to overcome every difficulty he might encounter in his progress, and to attain the object on which his heart was set.

His first step was to obtain a small set of chambers in Lincoln's Inn, and to begin, in good earnest, the study of jurisprudence.

A student, intended for the common law courts, was expected to work at least two years in the office of a special pleader, copying precedents, drawing declarations and pleas, and having an opportunity of seeing the run of his master's business. The most distinguished instructor in this line at that time was George Wood, in whose office Law, by great interest, obtained a desk.

The following letter, addressed to his friend Coxe, gives a lively notion of the young man's habits and sentiments at this period:—

"*June 18th*, 1773, TEMPLE, *Friday Night.*

"After holding a pen most of the day in the service of my profession, I will use it a few minutes longer in that of friendship. I thank you, my dearest friend, for this and every proof of confidence and affection. Let us cheerfully push our way in our different lines: the path of neither of us is strewed with roses, but they will terminate in happiness and honour. I cannot, however, now and then help sighing when I think how inglorious an apprenticeship we both of us serve to ambition—while you teach a child his rudiments, and I drudge at the pen for attorneys. But if knowledge and a respectable situation are to be purchased only on these terms, I, for my part can readily say 'hac mercede placet.' Do not commend my industry too soon; application wears for me at present the charm of novelty; upon a longer acquaintance I may grow tired of it."

It is not to be wondered at that a student just graduated at Cambridge, who had rejoiced in classical themes and associations, should at first find the study of the law dry and repulsive. In that study the labour is long, and the elements wearisome and uninteresting; but, we are assured by one whose experience had instructed him, "in the exquisite logic of special pleading, rightly understood, there is much to gratify an acute and vigorous understanding."

Young Law continued working very hard as a special pleading pupil for two years, during which period he became a great favourite with his instructor, and attracted the favourable attention of the attorneys who frequented Mr. Wood's chambers. When the time of his pupilage ceased he wisely determined not to be immediately called to the bar, but to commence "special pleader under the bar," sacrificing the chance of present éclat, and confining himself entirely to chamber practice, drawing law papers and giving opinions to the attorneys in cases of smaller consequence. "During five long and irksome years he continued to devote himself to this drudgery, (says his biographer), but his perseverance was amply rewarded, for he not only gained a reputation which was sure to start him with full business at the bar, but he acquired a thorough knowledge of his craft which few possess, who, after a mere course of solitary study, plunge into forensic wrangling."

In Hilary Term, 1780, he was called to the Bar by the Hon. Society of Lincoln's Inn. On the very day of his call he had several retainers given to him by great Northern attorneys; and from family connection, and his reputation as a special pleader, he reckoned he must speedily be at the head of the great Northern Circuit. In the beginning of March, he made his début at York, and appeared at the opening of the Nisi Prius court, with a large pile of papers lying before him. He was also provided with a bag—an honour of which no junior could ever before boast on his first circuit.*

The assizes being over, Mr. Law returned to London well pleased with his success and his prospects. During seven years he continued pursuing, with great ability and increasing reputation, the course on which he had entered; at the end of that period he pretty nearly monopolized the business of the six counties which form the Great Northern Circuit, and it was judged desirable that he should "have silk," a promotion which he attained in 1787. Shortly after this time he married the only daughter of Mr. Towry, a commissioner of the navy, a lady of great beauty and possessing a considerable

* "Now-a-days any young barrister buys a bag, and carries it as soon after he is called to the bar as he likes; but when I was called to the bar, and long after, the privilege of carrying a bag was strictly confined to those who had received one from a King's counsel. The King's counsel, then few in number, were considered officers of the crown, and they not only had a salary of £40 a year, but an annual allowance of paper, pens, and purple bags. These they distributed among juniors, who had made such progress as not to be able to carry their briefs conveniently in their hands."—*Lord Campbell in loc.*

fortune. She was born to be the wife of a great lawyer, being descended, on the mother's side, from Sir Thomas More, and is described as having been so singularly lovely that passers by would linger to watch her as she watered the flowers in the balcony of their house in Bloomsbury Square. The marriage was a truly happy one, and crowned with a numerous family, several of whom combined their father's talents with their mother's comeliness.

But, though supreme within the limits of the Northern Circuit, Mr. Law was unknown in the Law courts of London. Scarcely had he been employed in a single cause of interest there, and he panted for a fair opportunity to display his powers, believing that he wanted but this to become distinguished in the Court of King's Bench. How great must have been his surprise and delight when he found, one evening at his chamber, a general retainer from Warren Hastings, Esq., with a fee of five hundred guineas! At once he perceived that his fortune was made, and anticipated the satisfaction of his friends, and his own triumph, when entering the lists against such antagonists as Burke, Fox, and Sheridan, and the honours of the profession which he must eventually reap. What a high and arduous task for a young man of only eight years' standing at the bar, to lead the cause of the defendant in a trial of such unprecedented magnitude and interest! It appears that he owed this unexpected good fortune to the friendly representations of his kinsman, Sir Thomas Rumbold, who had been in office under the impeached governor in India, and mentioned Mr. Law in such high terms of praise as proved successful in procuring him the retainer.

This famous case—called by the illustrious Lord Brougham "the opprobrium of English justice, and, through mismanagement and party violence, the destruction of the greatest remedy afforded by our constitution, the impeachment of public wrong-doers"—commenced in the month of February 1788. In the mean time our lawyer had been preparing himself for the task he had undertaken with the utmost diligence. "Carrying along with him masses of despatches, examinations, and reports, which might have loaded many camels, he retreated to a cottage near the Lake of Windermere, and there spent a long vacation more laborious than the busiest term he had ever known in London."

At length the preparations for the trial were complete, and on the 13th February the sittings of the Court commenced. The scene has been depicted by the magical pen of Macaulay, and if any of my readers be acquainted with his description, I am sure he will be glad to read it again.

"There have been spectacles more dazzling to the eye, more gorgeous with jewellery and cloth of gold, more attractive to grown-up children than that which was then exhibited at Westminster; but perhaps there never was a spectacle so well calculated to strike a highly cultivated, a reflecting, an imaginative mind. All the various kinds of interest which belong to the near and to the distant, to the present and to the past, were collected on one spot and in one hour. All the talents and all the accomplishments which are developed by liberty and civilization were now displayed with every advantage that could be derived both from co-operation and from contrast. Every step in the proceedings carried the mind either backward, through many troubled centuries, to the days when the foundations of our constitution were laid; or far away, over boundless seas and deserts, to dusky nations living under strange stars, worshipping strange gods, and writing strange characters, from right to left. The High Court of Parliament was to sit, according to forms handed down from the days of the Plantagenets, on an Englishman accused of exercising tyranny over the lord of the holy city of Benares, and over the ladies of the princely house of Oude.

"The place was worthy of such a trial. It was the great hall of William Rufus, the hall which had resounded with acclamations at the inauguration of thirty kings, the hall which had witnessed the just sentence of Bacon, and the just absolution of Somers, the hall where the eloquence of Strafford had for a moment awed and melted a victorious party inflamed with just resentment, the hall where Charles had confronted the High Court of Justice with the placid courage which has half redeemed his fame. Neither military nor civil pomp was wanting. The avenues were lined with grenadiers. The streets were kept clear by cavalry. The peers, robed in gold and ermine, were marshalled by the heralds under Garter-King-at-arms. The judges, in their vestments of state, attended to give advice on points of law. Near a hundred and seventy lords, three-fourths of the Upper House as the Upper House then was, walked in solemn order from their usual place of assembling to the tribunal. The long procession was closed by the Duke of Norfolk, Earl Marshal of the realm, by the great dignitaries, and by the brothers and sons of the King. Last of all came the Prince of Wales, conspicuous by his fine person and noble bearing. The gray old walls were hung with scarlet. The long galleries were crowded by an audience such as has rarely excited the fears or the emulation of an orator. There were gathered together, from all parts of a great, free, enlightened, and prosperous empire, grace and female loveliness, wit and learning, the representatives of every science and of every art. There were seated round the Queen the fair-haired young daughters of the house of Brunswick. There the ambassadors of great kings and commonwealths gazed with admiration on a spectacle which no other country in the world could present. . . . .

"The serjeants made proclamation. Hastings advanced to the bar and bent his knee. The culprit was indeed not unworthy of that great presence. He had ruled an extensive and populous country; had made laws and treaties; had sent forth armies and pulled down princes. And in this high place he had so borne himself that all had feared him, that most had loved him, and that hatred itself could deny him no title to glory except virtue. He looked like a great man, and not like a bad man. A person small and emaciated, yet deriving dignity from a carriage which, while it indicated deference to the court, indicated also habitual self-possession and self-respect, a high and intellectual forehead, a brow pensive but not gloomy, a mouth of inflexible decision, a face pale and worn but serene, on which was written, as legibly as under the picture in the Council Chamber at Calcutta, *Mens æqua in arduis;* such was the aspect with which the great proconsul presented himself to his judges.

"His counsel accompanied him; men all of whom were

afterwards raised by their talents and learning to the highest posts in their profession, the bold and strong minded Law, afterwards Chief Justice of the King's Bench; the more humane and eloquent Dallas, afterwards Chief-Justice of the Common Pleas; and Plomer, who, near twenty years later, successfully conducted in the same court the defence of Lord Melville, and subsequently became Vice-Chancellor and Master of the Rolls.

"But neither the culprit nor his advocates attracted so much notice as the accusers. In the midst of the blaze of red drapery a space had been fitted up with green benches and tables for the Commons. The managers, with Burke at their head, appeared in full dress. The collectors of gossip did not fail to remark that even Fox, generally so regardless of his appearance, had paid to the illustrious tribunal the compliment of wearing a bag and sword. The box in which the managers stood contained an array of speakers such as perhaps had not appeared together since the great age of Athenian eloquence. There were Fox and Sheridan, the English Demosthenes and the English Hyperides. There was Burke, ignorant, indeed, or negligent of the art of adapting his reasonings and his style to the capacity and taste of his hearers, but in amplitude of comprehension and richness of imagination superior to every orator, ancient or modern. There, with eyes reverentially fixed on Burke, appeared the finest gentleman of the age, the ingenious, the chivalrous, the high-souled Windham. Nor, though surrounded by such men, did the youngest manager pass unnoticed. . . . . He is the sole representative of a great age which has passed away. Those who, within the last ten years, have listened with delight, till the morning sun shone on the tapestries of the House of Lords, to the lofty and animated eloquence of Charles, Earl Grey, are able to form some estimate of the powers of a race of men, among whom he was not the foremost." *

To combat, with any hope of success, so formidable an array of professional talent, seconded by such a world of eloquence and rhetoric, required strong nerves, readiness of mind, perfect self-possession, and undaunted energy, and, happily for his client, Mr. Law possessed the requisite courage and ability. No wonder that, at first, he appears to have been daunted by the strangeness and grandeur of the scene and by his appreciation of the matchless powers of intellect and oratory opposed to him, to such a degree as to manifest symptoms of timidity, and to look pale and alarmed, while his voice trembled. But this emotion, after he had somewhat become accustomed to his novel position, subsided, and he acquitted himself so as to obtain the highest approbation of the great men in whose presence he appeared. "I have been so fortunate," says Lord Brougham, "as to obtain the shorthand writer's notes of Mr. Law's celebrated Defence of Hastings, and a careful perusal of it has fully satisfied me that its merits fully answer its reputation, and that his great forensic powers have not been overrated by the general opinion of Westminster Hall. There is a lucid order in the statement of his details, struggling as he did with the vast compass and repulsive materials of his subject, and a plain, manly vigour in the argument, far more valuable to his cause than any

* Lord Macaulay's Essays, vol. iii. 445.

rhetorical display. But there is also much of the purest and most effective eloquence. The topics and the illustrations are felicitously chosen; the occasional figures are chastely but luminously introduced; the diction is pure and nervous, marked by the love of strong and homely phrase which was breathed in his discourse; the finer passages have rarely been surpassed by any effort of forensic power, must have produced a great effect under all the disadvantages of an exhausted auditory and a worn out controversy, and would have ranked with the most successful exhibitions of the oratorical art had they been delivered in the early stage of the trial."

Not until the 23d of April, 1795, being the one hundred and forty-fifth day of the trial, and in the tenth year from the commencement of the crimination did this celebrated impeachment close, when the first counsel for the accused had the satisfaction to hear his client acquitted by a large majority of Peers, and was himself warmly congratulated by his friends upon the happy event.

Mr. Law's fees, amounting to upwards of £3000, were but an inadequate compensation for his exertions and sacrifices in this great cause; but he was amply rewarded by the increase of his reputation and consequent access of business. The highest walks of the bar were soon opened to him; and from this time he was regarded as second only to the wondrous master of eloquence, Erskine.

To his professional success was afterwards added the political promotion which he had long awaited. In 1801 he was made Attorney-General, was knighted by George III., and was returned to Parliament, where he did not, however, distinguish himself. Soon after, Lord Kenyon's death made way for him on the bench, and he was, at the same time, raised to the peerage. Of his qualifications as a judge his biographer speaks in high praise. He was particularly famous for mercantile law, and by his practice under the bar had become familiarly versed in all the intricacies of special pleading. "When his powerful mind was brought to bear upon any question that came before him, whether sitting alone at Nisi Prius, or with his brethren in Banco, the impression which he made upon it was immediate, sure, and deep," says Lord Brougham. He adds, "He was sometimes irascible, and occasionally even violent. But no one could accuse him of the least partiality; his honest and manly nature ever disdained as much to trample overbearingly on the humble, as to crouch meanly before the powerful. He was sometimes impatient; and, as his mind was rather strong than nimble, he often betrayed hastiness of conclusion more than he displayed quickness of apprehension. On the bench it is not to be denied that Lord Ellenborough occasionally suffered the strength of his political feelings to break forth, and to influence the tone and temper of his observations. That he ever, upon any one occasion, knowingly deviated one hair's breadth from justice in the discharge of his office, is wholly untrue."

Lord Campbell's lively pages relate, with evident gusto, some of the sarcastic effusions in which Lord Ellenborough indulged from the Bench, and by which he acquired renown among the habitués of Westminster Hall. A few of these may be given here. On one occasion a witness, dressed in a fantastical manner, having given very rambling and discreditable evidence, was asked, in cross-examination, what he was. *Witness.*—"I employ myself as a surgeon." *Lord Ellenborough, C. J.*—"But, does any one else *employ you as a surgeon?*"

A great sessions lawyer, but known as a dreadful *bore*, was arguing a question upon the rateability of certain quarries to the relief of the poor, and contended at enormous length that, "like lead and copper mines, they were not rateable because the limestone in them could only be reached by deep *boring*, which was matter of science." *Lord Ellenborough, C. J.*—"You will hardly succeed in convincing us, sir, that every species of *boring* is '*matter of science.*'"

A declamatory speaker, who despised all technicalities, and tried to storm the court by the force of eloquence, was once, when uttering these words, "In the book of nature, my Lords, it is written—" stopped by this question from the Chief-Justice, "Will you have the goodness to mention the page, sir, if you please?"

Towards the end of Easter Term, a tiresome conveyancer having occupied the whole day about the *merger of a term*, the Chief Justice said to him, "I am afraid, sir, the Term, although a long one, will *merge* in your argument."

A very tedious bishop having yawned during his own speech, Lord Ellenborough exclaimed, "Come, come, the fellow shows some symptoms of taste, but this is encroaching upon our province."

At the coming in of the "Talents" in 1806, Erskine himself pressed the Great Seal upon Ellenborough, saying that "he would add to the splendour of his reputation as Lord Chancellor." Ellenborough, knowing that on his own refusal Erskine was to be the man, exclaimed, "How can you ask me to accept the office of Lord Chancellor, when I know as little of its duties as you do?"

Although thus he frequently indulged in sharp sayings, he was acquitted of any malignant disposition, since it was evident he spoke from a love of fun, and he had in him a large stock of good humour and *bon-hommie*, which made him a very pleasant and entertaining companion.

In domestic life his lordship was exceedingly amiable, very rarely yielding to his natural hastiness of temper. On one occasion it appears he paid, by his own discomfiture, for a little domestic irritability. The tale used to be told by Mr. Rogers, as follows:—

"Lord Ellenborough was once about to go on the circuit, when Lady Ellenborough said she should like to accompany him. He replied that he had no objection, provided that she did not encumber the carriage with bandboxes, which were his utter abhorrence. During the first day's journey, Lord Ellenborough, happening to stretch his legs, struck his foot against something below the seat. He discovered that it was a bandbox. Up went the window, and out went the bandbox. The coachman stopped, and the footmen, thinking that the bandbox had tumbled out of the window by some extraordinary chance, were going to pick it up, when Lord Ellenborough called out furiously, 'Drive on!' The bandbox was accordingly left by the ditch side. Having reached the county town where he was to officiate as judge, his lordship proceeded to array himself for his appearance in the court house. 'Now,' said he, 'where's my wig—where *is* my wig?' 'My lord,' replied his attendant, 'it was thrown out of the carriage window.'"

In person Lord Ellenborough was above the middle size, but ungraceful, and his walk singularly awkward. His portrait by Sir Thomas Lawrence gives a favourable and impressive representation of him, portraying correctly his broad, commanding brow, his projecting eyebrows, dark and shaggy, his stern black eyes, and the deep lines of thought that marked his countenance. His robust, though ungainly frame, presented an appearance of great strength, until shattered by disease. His labours had been truly enormous, and proved too severe a burden for even his iron frame. Symptoms of decay began to exhibit themselves before he had reached an advanced age, and he found himself compelled to retire from public life. He did not long survive the excitement of office, and expired on the 13th December 1818, in the sixty-ninth year of his age. For some time before his resignation, he appears to have had a serious foreboding that his earthly career was drawing to a close, and, during a visit he made to Paris in the autumn before his death, he composed the following beautiful prayer, indicative of a Christian's hope, combined with pious thankfulness and humble resignation:—

"O God, heavenly Father, by whose providence and goodness all things were made and have their being, and from whom all the blessings and comforts of this life, and all the hopes and expectations of happiness hereafter, are, through the merits of our blessed Saviour, derived to us Thy sinful creatures, I humbly offer up my most grateful thanks and acknowledgments for Thy divine goodness and protection, constantly vouchsafed to me through the whole course of my life, particularly in indulging to me such faculties of mind and body, and such means of health and strength, as have hitherto enabled me to obtain and to enjoy many great worldly comforts and advantages.

"Grant me, O Lord, I humbly beseech Thee, a due sense of these, Thy manifold blessings, together with a steadfast disposition and purpose to use them for the benefit of my fellow-creatures, and Thy honour and glory. And grant, O Lord, that no decay or diminution of these faculties and means of happiness may excite in my mind any dissatisfied or desponding thoughts or feelings, but that I may always place my firm trust and confidence in Thy divine goodness. And, whether the blessings heretofore indulged to me shall be continued or cease, and whether Thou shalt give them or take them away, I may still, in humble obedience to Thy divine will, submit myself in all things with patience and resignation to the dispensations of Thy divine providence, humbly and gratefully blessing, praising, and magnifying Thy holy name for ever and ever.—Amen.

"PARIS, 1817."

XI.

Lord Eldon.

IT is not easy to imagine a more lawyer-like cautious record than the following, "I was born, I believe, on the 4th June, 1751." This is the first entry in a MS. book, written by the celebrated Lord Eldon in his latter years for the amusement and information of his grandson, and the autobiographical notices there given contain many entertaining anecdotes of this great lawyer and remarkable individual. He was the younger son of Mr. William Scott, a worthy, industrious and prudent man, who carried on the business of a coal-fitter at Newcastle-upon-Tyne. His mother, Jane, the daughter of Mr. Atkinson, a tradesman of the same town, is said to have been remarkable for shrewdness and superior ability. She had a very numerous family, two of whom attained to eminence,—the eldest, William, afterwards Lord Stowell; and John, nearly six years his junior, the future Lord Eldon.

As soon as they were old enough the two brothers were sent, successively, to the Free Grammar School at Newcastle, and one of the first pages of the "Anecdote Book" contains this affectionate remembrance of their early instructor:—"The head-master was that eminent scholar and most excellent man, the Rev. Mr. Moises. I shall hold his memory in the utmost veneration, whilst I continue to exist. There were also excellent ushers in that school whilst I continued in it. I gratefully mention the names of Mr. Clarkson, Mr. Hall, Mr. King, and Mr. Walters." Both William and John were diligent scholars and great favourites with their master, but they were widely different in character, and even at that early period the distinctive peculiarities of their minds were shown. It is related that when asked to give an account of the Sunday sermon—their father's weekly custom—the eldest would repeat a sort of digest of the general argument, a condensed summary of what he had heard; John, on the other hand, would recapitulate the minutiæ of the discourse, and reiterate the very phrase of the preacher. He showed a memory the most complete and exact; but failed in giving the whole scope and clear general view of the sermon, embodied in half the number of words by the elder brother.

Although very diligent in his studies, the future Lord Chancellor was, according to his own account, much given to play idle pranks out of school hours. Several of these he has related; among others, the following:—'I remember stealing, with a playmate, down the Side and along the Sandhill, and creeping into every shop, where we blew out the candles. We crept in along the counter, then pop't our heads up, out went the candles, and away went we. We escaped detection." Many other practical jokes he indulged in, and some of a more objectionable kind. To his solicitor, Mr. Chisholme, he gave the following grave piece of evidence against his own juvenile character:—"My father," said he, "agreed with a master who kept a writing-school to teach me the art of penmanship there, for half a guinea a quarter. In the whole of the three months, I attended that school but once. My father knew nothing of this, and at the quarter's end gave me half a guinea to pay the master. When I took it to the school, the master said he did not know how he could properly receive it, since he had given nothing in exchange for it. I said that he really must take it; that I could not possibly carry it back to my father. 'Well,' replied he, 'if I am to take it, at all events I must give something for it: so come here.' And, upon my going up to him, he took the money with one hand, and with the other gave me—a box on the ear, which sent me reeling against the wainscot;—and that was the way I first learned to write."

Every admirer of Bewick's genius will be reminded of him by the next anecdote, for he has, in one of the inimitable "tail-pieces" of his "History of British Birds," depicted to the very life the boyish pastime in which the embryo judge delighted:—"Between school-hours we used to amuse ourselves with playing at what we called '*cock nibs*,' that was, riding on grave-stones in St. John's church-yard, which, you know, was close to the school. Well, one day, one of the lads came shouting, 'Here comes Moises'—that's what we always called him, Moises—so away we all ran as hard as we could, and I lost my hat; at which my father was very angry, and he made me go without one till the usual time of taking my best into every-day wear." One of the ladies of the family added to this story, "On this occasion Lord Eldon went three months, Sundays excepted, without a hat."

His next exploit, and for which he was carried before a magistrate, was robbing an orchard, or, as the boys called it, "boxing the fox." "There were three of us. The magistrate acted upon what I think was rather curious law, for he fined our fathers each thirty shillings for our offence. *We* did not care for that, but then *they did:* so my father flogged me, and then sent a message to Moises, and Moises flogged me again. We were very good boys; very good boys, indeed; we never did anything worse than a robbery."

Thus in after days he told "the follies of his youth;" but chiefly it pleased him to recall to mind his early gallantries:—"I believe," he said to his niece, Mrs. Forster, "no shoemaker ever helped to put on more ladies' shoes than I have done. At the dancing school the young ladies always brought their dancing-shoes with them, and we deemed it a proper piece of etiquette to assist the pretty girls in putting them on. In those days girls of the best families wore white stockings only on the Sundays, and one week day which was a sort of public day; on the other days they wore blue Doncaster woollen stockings with white tags.

"We used, when we were at the Head School, early on the Sunday mornings, to steal flowers from the gardens in the neighbourhood of the Forth, and then we presented them to our sweethearts. Oh, these were happy days—we were always in love then."

School-days fly all too swiftly away, and the merry, fun-loving boy becomes the shy and awkward lad. Then comes the posing question, What is to be done with him? Young John Scott had nearly reached the age of fifteen when his worthy father began to consider that matter, and arrived at the conclusion that the best thing would be to bind him apprentice to his own trade as a coal-fitter; but before taking the final step he mentioned his intention to William, his eldest son, who was then at the University of Oxford; "Send Jack up to me," was his answer, "I can do better for him here." And he was sent accordingly, and duly became a Commoner of University College. "I was entered," he notes in his book, "under the tuition of Sir R. Chambers, and my brother Lord Stowell." He then wanted a few weeks of fifteen, and was so small of his age that he looked a mere boy.

Very pleasant is the account he himself has given of his first launch from off the native perch into the big world in which he was destined to make, during his little day of life, a somewhat conspicuous figure. "I have seen it remarked," he says, "that something which in early youth captivates attention influences future life in all its stages. When I left school in 1766 to go to Oxford, I came up from Newcastle to London in a coach, then denominated, on account of its quick travelling, as travelling was then estimated, a fly; being as well as I remember, nevertheless, three or four days and nights on the road. On the panels of the coach were painted the words, '*Sat cito, si sat bene;*' words which made a most lasting impression on my mind, and have had their influence upon my conduct in all subsequent life. Their effect was heightened by circumstances that occurred during and immediately after the journey.

"Upon the journey a Quaker, who was a fellow-traveller, stopped the coach at the inn at Tuxford, desired the chambermaid to come to the coach door and gave her a sixpence, telling her he forgot to give it her when he slept there two years before. I was a very saucy boy and said to him, 'Friend, have you seen the motto on the coach?' 'No.' 'Then look at it; for I think giving her only sixpence *now*, is neither *sat cito* nor *sat bene.*'

"After I got to town my brother met me at the White Horse in Fetter Lane, Holborn, then the great Oxford house, as I was told. He took me to see the play at Drury Lane. When we came out of the house it rained hard. There were then few hackney-coaches, and we got both into one sedan-chair. Turning out of Fleet Street into Fetter Lane, there was a sort of contest between our chairmen and some persons who were coming up Fleet Street. In the struggle the sedan chair was overset with us in it. This, thought I, is more than *sat cito*, and it certainly is not *sat bene.* In short, in all that I have had to do in life, professional and judicial, I have always felt the effect of this early admonition."

He had not been many weeks at Oxford when the long vacation arrived, and he was sent back by his judicious father to school, to continue his studies there in the interim; "a sad pull-down," said he, "to my dignity." In the autumn he returned to his Alma Mater, where he remained as undergraduate three years; at the age of sixteen he was elected a Fellow of his college, an honour which he ascribed entirely to his brother's influence.

William Scott was born, by a fortunate accident, as it afterwards proved, in the county of Durham, and by this fortuitous circumstance the destiny of both brothers was materially affected. His mother was alarmed by the approach of the rebel army in 1745, and being near her confinement, retreated to her husband's country house a few miles distant from Newcastle, and situate in the county of Durham. Taking advantage of this accidental qualification, the wonderfully precocious lad became a candidate for the Fellowship in Oxford which he afterwards obtained. By his influence the same advantage was secured for his younger brother, and to both, said Lord Eldon, "these fellowships were of great use in life and in our subsequent success. We owe much, therefore, to what it is to be wished nobody should profit by, namely, rebellion."

The young collegian took his B.A. degree on the 20th February, 1770. This was a very different affair to what it is in our day. According to his account an examination for a degree at Oxford was then a mere farce. He was examined in Hebrew and in history. "What is the Hebrew for the place of a skull?" He replied, "Golgotha." "Who founded University College?" He stated that "King Alfred founded it." "Very well, sir," said the examiner, "you are competent for your degree."

In the following year his prize essay, "On the Advantages and Disadvantages of Foreign Travel," was adjudged to bear the palm, and his success was hailed with delight by his friends in Newcastle, most of all by his old preceptor, who on receiving the tidings rushed into the school with a copy of the essay in his hand, exclaiming, "See, boys, what Jack Scott has done."

To this early triumph Lord Eldon used, in later years, to recur with undisguised pride and satisfaction, dwelling upon the encouragement it gave him at the time, acting as a spur to future exertion. When entering the theatre on the eventful day of the contest he drew back from feelings of diffidence and modesty, and his friend the Bishop of Clonfert was obliged "to take him by the shoulders and push him forward," he hesitated so much about venturing in.

It should seem this success emboldened him to take a rash step, and one which at the time was regarded by his friends as subversive of all his prospects and bright hopes for the future. It was the old, old story, love at first sight—

> "The mutual flame, so quickly caught,
> And quickly, too, revealed;"

followed by opposition on the part of prudent relatives, and difficulties threatening to part the lovers; and then, that summary method of cutting such a gordian knot—a runaway marriage.

The object of the youth's attachment was the lovely daughter of Mr. Surtees, a banker in Newcastle, and whose portrait is thus pleasantly drawn by one of her relations: "Her figure was slight and of a short middle size. Her hair, of the deepest brown, streamed in rich ringlets over her neck. From her mother—the beauty of a preceding generation, she had inherited features of an exquisite regularity as well as a strongly marked character, and a warm temper."

The youthful pair—very young indeed they were; he was but just of age, and she had hardly completed her eighteenth year—conducted their affair in the approved fashion: "On the night of the 18th Nov. 1772, Miss Surtees, 'having made up her mind to a decisive measure,' descended by a ladder into the arms of her lover, from a window of her father's house in the Sandhill, Newcastle;" and after narrowly escaping discovery the runaways reached their postchaise safely, crossed the Border that night, and were married the following morning at the village of Blackshiels, in Scotland.

Great was the consternation of their respective families when they learned what had taken place; "Jack Scott has run off with Bessie Surtees, and the poor lad is undone," exclaimed the worthy Moises; and his nearest relations shared the same grievous forebodings. "I suppose you have heard of this very foolish act of my very foolish brother," said Mr. William Scott, to a mutual friend, "he is completely ruined, nor can anything now save him from beggary; you do not know how unhappy this makes me; for I had good hopes of him till this last absurd step has destroyed all." On their part the sisters of the rash bridegroom acted as women commonly do on such occasions. They had been let into the secret on the previous evening, and sobbed and cried all night long; then, drying their eyes, they looked the next morning at breakfast with anxious glances at their father, while he read, in gloomy silence, a letter from the culprit.

In the meantime Mr. and Mrs. John Scott were awaiting the result of this epistle with no small impatience. They stayed at an hotel in Morpeth for two or three days, uncertain and expectant. The bride, it is said, used to describe this interval as passed very miserably. Their funds were exhausted, they had no home to go to, and they knew not what reception they should meet with from their friends. In this sad state of things she suddenly espied from the window of their room a fine large wolf-dog called Loup, walking along the street; a joyful sight, for she felt sure that a friend was at hand; and in a few minutes Henry Scott, a third brother, entered the room, bringing with him a message of forgiveness and an invitation to Love Lane, which was most gladly accepted. Not long after, the two fathers of the newly-married pair agreed to allow them jointly a small income for present necessities, and then John Scott was cast on his own resources, and "having," as he says in his Anecdote Book, "the world before me, and as it proved, a most kind providence my guide, I gave up the purpose of taking orders, and entered as a student in the Middle Temple, in January 1773."

Shortly after his marriage, Mr. John Scott, writing to a fellow-collegian, said: "I have married rashly, and have neither house nor home to offer my wife; but it is my determination to work hard to provide for the woman I love as soon as I can find the means of doing so." And to this purpose he adhered with unflinching diligence and self-denial. For the greater part of three years which must elapse before he could be called to the Bar, he continued to live in or near Oxford, and his eldest son, John, was born at New Inn Hall in the month of March 1774. Among his anecdotes of this period are the following. "The most awkward thing that ever occurred to me was this: immediately after I was married I was appointed Deputy Professor of Law at Oxford, and the law professor sent me the first lecture, which I had to read *immediately* to the students, and which I began without knowing a single word that was in it. It was upon the statute of young men running away with maidens. Fancy me reading with about one hundred and forty boys and young men, all giggling at the professor. Such a tittering audience no one ever had."

"The first cause I ever decided was an apple pie cause. I was a senior fellow at University College, and two of the undergraduates came to complain to me that the cook had sent them an apple pie that *could not be eaten.* So I said I would hear both sides. I summoned the cook to make his defence, who said that he never had anything unfit for the table, and that there was then a remarkably fine fillet of veal in the kitchen. Now here we were at fault; for I could not understand what a fillet of veal in the kitchen had to do with an apple pie in the hall. So that I might come to a right understanding of the merits of the case, I ordered the pie itself to be brought before me. The messenger returned and informed me that the other undergraduates had taken advantage of the absence of the two complainants and had eaten the whole of the apple pie; so you know it was impossible for me to decide that *that* was not eatable which was actually eaten. I have often wished in after life that all the causes were apple pie causes; fine easy work it would have been."

During his probationary three years he had to visit London periodically, for the purpose of keeping his terms, and on one of these occasions the following amusing incident occurred:—Mr. Serjeant Hill, a most learned lawyer, but a very eccentric man, stopped him in the hall of the Middle Temple, and said, "Pray, young gentleman, do you think herbage and pannage rateable to the poor's rate?" He answered, "Sir, I cannot presume to give any opinion, inexperienced and unlearned as I am, to a person of your great knowledge and high character in the profession." "Upon my word," said the Serjeant, "you are a pretty sensible young gentleman: I don't often meet with such. If I had asked Mr. Burgess, a young man upon our circuit, the question, he would have told me that I was an old fool. You are an extraordinary sensible young gentleman."

So severe was the labour to which he now submitted himself, that before long it began to tell upon his health, and his cadaverous looks awakened the anxiety of his friends. One of them, a physician, remonstrated and urged the necessity of some abatement in the severity of his application. "It is no matter," was his reply, "I must do as I am now doing, or starve." Accordingly he read with pertinacious zeal, rising at the early hour of four in the morning, observed a careful abstinence at his meals, and that he might drive away the oppressive drowsiness which interfered with his studies at night, wrapped a wet towel round his head. When he was an old man he recurred to these days as not unhappy, though so laborious. At length, in the long vacation of 1775, he bade adieu to Oxford, and moved with his little family to a small house in Cursitor Street, near Chancery Lane. Pointing to this house in his days of prosperity he would say, "There was my first perch. Many a time have I run down from Cursitor Street to Fleet Market to buy sixpenn'orth of sprats for our supper." He received at this juncture the kindly assistance of an eminent conveyancer, into whose office he was admitted without remuneration. This was Mr. Duane, a Roman Catholic, and a most worthy and excellent man. Lord Eldon loved to refer to this act of liberality, saying, "It was a great kindness to me. The knowledge I acquired of conveyancing in his office was of infinite service during a long life in the Court of Chancery." Throughout the six months agreed upon he worked almost night and day, and to supply the deficiency arising from his never having been with any special pleader or equity draughtsman, he copied all the MS. forms he could lay his hand upon. Two large volumes compiled in this manner he afterwards lost. He supposed he had lent them to some forgetful borrower; and of such delinquents would sometimes say, "Though backward in *accounting*, they seem to be practised *in book-keeping*."

For several years he found it very uphill-work, and afterwards used to relate his troubles when climbing the ladder, thus making his subsequent success the more telling. "When first I was called to the Bar," he would say, "Bessy and I thought all our troubles were over; business was to pour in, and we were to be almost rich immediately." Alas! these golden dreams were quickly dissipated; during the first year he received but one half guinea, of which one shilling and sixpence went for fees! But he had a never-failing solace in his darkest hours of discouragement in the loving devotedness of his wife, who was his constant companion, accustomed herself to his hours, and would sit up with him far into the night, silently watching his studies, and moving cautiously lest she should disturb or interrupt him. Her affection for him was something touching to witness, and it was repaid by the deep, earnest, and enduring love he bore her. After a happy union of almost forty years he thus addressed her on the anniversary of their marriage:—

"Can it, my lovely Bessy, be
That when near forty years are past

I still my much-loved charmer see
Dearer and dearer at the last?

Nor time, nor years, nor age, nor care,
Believe me, lovely Bessy, will—
Much as this frame they daily wear—
Affect the heart that's faithful still."

If these lines prove the great law lord—then Chancellor of England—was not gifted with poetic genius, they speak of something better even than that, and one's heart warms with a feeling of kindly regard toward him which would never have been awakened by anything independent of the personal character and domestic excellence of the man. It is these endearing relationships of life that produce and cherish true worth, and are the appointed providential means of perpetuating all that is good and lovely in the families of men upon the earth.

In his later years, we are told, Lord Eldon recurred to the period of his poverty and obscurity as the happiest of his life: for then, he said, "we were all in all to each other, and she did many things for me which have never been so well done since." There were fond attentions none could pay as she did, cutting his hair, arranging his linen and clothes for dress, and stealing to the window when he went out to watch him as he passed by.

Yet, notwithstanding this sweet drop in the cup, he was not insensible to the discouragements that he endured from the long delay in his professional rise. "Business is very dull with poor Jack," wrote his kind and ever-watchful brother; "and in consequence he is not very lively; I heartily wish that it may brisken a little, else he will be heartily sick of his profession." In fact, the "hope deferred" brought on such continued low spirits that his health began to be seriously undermined.

He consulted an eminent physician, who sent him to Bath in the expectation that the waters would bring on a crisis of his disorder, as in fact proved to be the case, and he came back improved. He used to tell that, when he put his hand in his pocket to give the doctor his fee, he was stopped with the question, "Are you the young gentleman who gained the prize for the essay at Oxford? Then I shall take no fee from you."

The Anecdote Book contains many stories of the incidents that occurred to him when going the northern circuit, where it was long before he obtained adequate remuneration. One spring circuit he was absent from York and Lancaster, being, as he said, unable to afford the expense of attendance. It is related that the Rev. Sidney Smith, in an assize sermon preached in York Cathedral in 1824, said, for the encouragement of desponding young barristers, "Fifty years ago, the person at the head of the profession, the greatest lawyer now in England, perhaps in the world, stood in this church on such an occasion as the present, as obscure, as unknown, and as much doubting of his future prospects as the humblest individual of the profession here present."

But his time was at hand. At the very juncture when he was about to leave London in despair, and to settle as a provincial counsel in his native town, the tide turned in his favour; an admirable opportunity was afforded him for the exhibition of his extraordinary merit as a lawyer, and from that time his advancement was rapid and steady. The circumstances of the case were thus told by himself little more than three weeks before his death, to Mr. Farrer, the Master in Chancery, who was dining with him, and who inquired, "Whether Ackroyd *v.* Smithson was not the first cause in which he distinguished himself?" "Did I never tell you the history?" was his reply. "Come, help yourself to a glass of Newcastle port, and give me a little. You must know that the testator in that cause had directed his real estates to be sold, and, after paying his debts and funeral and testamentary expenses, the residue of the money to be divided into fifteen parts, which he gave to fifteen persons whom he named in his will. One of these persons died in the testator's life-time. A bill was filed by the next of kin, claiming amongst other things the lapsed share. A brief was given me to consent for the heir at law, upon the hearing of the cause. I had nothing then to do but to pore over this brief. I went through all the cases in the books, and satisfied myself that the lapsed share was to be considered as real estate, and belonged to my client (the heir at law). The cause came on at the Rolls, before Sir Thomas Sewell. I told the solicitor who sent me the brief that I should consent for the heir at law, so far as regarded the due execution of the will, but that I must support the title of the heir to the one-fifteenth, which had lapsed. Accordingly I did argue it, and went through all the authorities. When Sir Thomas Sewell went out of the court, he asked the Register who that young man was? The Register told him it was Mr. Scott. 'He has argued very well,' said Sir Thomas Sewell, 'but I cannot agree with him.' This the Register told me. He decreed against my client.

"The cause having been carried, by appeal, to the Lord Chancellor Thurlow, a guinea fee was again brought to me to consent. I told my client if he meant by 'consent' to give up the claim of the heir to the lapsed share, he must take his brief elsewhere, for I would not hold it without arguing that point. He said something about young men being obstinate, but that I must do as I thought right. You see, the lucky thing was, there being *two* other parties, and, the disappointed one not being content, there was an appeal to Lord Thurlow.

"In the meanwhile they had written to Mr. Johnston, Recorder of York, guardian to the young heir at law, and a clever man, but his answer was, 'Do not send good money after bad: let Mr. Scott have a guinea to give consent, and if he will argue, why let him do so, but give him no more.'

"So I went into court, and when Lord Thurlow asked who was to appear for the heir at law, I rose, and said modestly, that I was; and as I could not but think (with much deference to the Master of the Rolls, for I might be wrong), that my client had the right to the property, if his lordship would give me leave I would argue it.

"It was rather arduous for me to rise against all the eminent counsel. I do not say that their *opinions* were against me; but they were *employed* against me. However, I argued that the testator had ordered this fifteenth share of the property to be converted into personal property, for the benefit of one particular individual, and that therefore he never contemplated its coming into possession of either the next of kin or the residuary legatee; but, being land at the death of the individual, it came to the heir at law. Well, Thurlow took three days to consider, and then delivered his judgment in accordance with my speech, and that speech is in print, and has decided all similar questions ever since.

"As I left the hall, a respectable solicitor of the name of Forster, came up and touched me on the shoulder, and said, 'Young man, your bread and butter is cut for life,' or, 'you have cut your bread and butter.'

"But the story of *Ackroyd* v. *Smithson* does not stop there. In the Chancellor's Court of Lancaster, where Dunning (Lord Ashburton) was Chancellor, a brief was given me in a cause in which the interest of my client would oblige me to support by argument the reverse of that which had been decided by the decree in *Ackroyd* v. *Smithson*. When I had stated to the court the point I was going to argue, Dunning said, 'Sit down, young man.' As I did not immediately comply, he repeated, 'Sit down, sir; I won't hear you.' I then sat down. Dunning said, 'I believe your name is Scott, sir.' I said that it was. Upon which he went on—'Mr. Scott, did you not argue that case of Ackroyd *v.* Smithson?' I said that I did argue it. He then said, 'Mr. Scott, I have read your argument in that case, and I defy you or any man in England to answer it. I won't hear you.'"

It is no wonder that this argument made a great sensation in Westminster Hall. From that day the happy and deservedly successful debutant took rank among those greatly envied lawyers who—

> "From morn to night at Senate, Rolls, and Hall,
> Plead much, read more, dine late, or not at all."

With diligence, ability, and usefulness he worked his upward way, the door being now open to him, which was, in fact, all he had needed. In a short time, as he was found to be rapidly getting into the lead, a silk gown was offered to him without solicitation; and, soon after, he was returned to Parliament, under the auspices of

Lord Thurlow, who thenceforward was his steady friend and patron, while, from his circuit and town practice, he began to count a yearly saving, which at length accumulated to a princely fortune.

Here, then, having seen the future Lord Chancellor on the high road to wealth and distinction, we will take our leave of him; but, for the amusement of the reader, I shall add a few of the more characteristic and piquant anecdotes which he stored up, and, as long as he lived, delighted in his jocular hours to relate.

The Anecdote Book contained some amusing recollections belonging to the period of his official service. "When I was Solicitor or Attorney-General," said he, "we had this ingenious case of smuggling proved:—A person at Dover smuggled three thousand pairs of French gloves. He sent all the right-hand gloves to London. They were seized and sold. Nobody would buy right-hand gloves; the smuggler, therefore, bought them for a mere trifle. He then, having secured the right-hand gloves, sent the three thousand left-handed gloves to London. They were also seized, sold, and of course bought by him for a nominal price. Thus he became possessed of them, though contraband, according to law, and, as a smuggler would say, in an honest way."

At another time, a case was brought before him for the recovery of a dog, which the defendant had stolen, and detained from the plaintiff, its owner. "We had," said he, "a great deal of evidence, and the dog was brought into court, and placed on the table between the judge and witnesses. He was a very fine dog, very large and very fierce, so much so, that I ordered a muzzle to be put on it. Well, we could come to no decision, when a woman all in rags came forward, and said, if I would allow her to get into the witness-box, she thought she could say something that would decide the cause. Well, she was sworn just as she was, all rags and tatters, and leant forward towards the animal, and said, 'Come, Billy, come and kiss me!' The savage-looking dog instantly raised itself on its hind legs, put its immense paws around her neck, and saluted her. She had brought it up from a puppy. These words, 'Come, Billy, come and kiss me,' decided the cause."

Lord Eldon was very fond of dogs. He had a Newfoundland which, for many years, acted as guard at Encombe House, his country mansion; and for this animal he designed a tombstone, and wrote an elaborate inscription, recording its fidelity and attachment. But his great favourite, the constant companion of his latter days, was Pincher, a poodle dog, which had belonged to his eldest son, a most promising young man, who died in the prime of life. He used to caress this animal, and tell how his poor son, when he was *in extremis*, said, "Father, you will take care of poor Pincher." The dog was brought to his new master's house as soon as all was over. In a short time he was missed, and being immediately sought for, was found lying on the bed beside his dead master.

Pincher was often introduced into the portraits of the Chancellor, who said, "Poor fellow! he has a right to be painted with me, for when my man Smith took him the other day to a law bookseller's, where there were several lawyers assembled, they all received him with great respect; and the master of the shop exclaimed, 'How very like he is to *old Eldon*, particularly when he wore a wig!' But, indeed, many people say he is the better looking chap of the two!"

Lord Eldon used to relate many stories of the stupidity and incapacity of jurymen. "I remember," said he, "Mr. Justice Gould trying a cause at York; and when he had proceeded for about two hours, he observed, 'Here are only eleven jurymen in the box: where is the twelfth?'—'Please you, my lord,' said one of the eleven, 'he is gone away about some business; but he has left his verdict with me.' At another time, coming down the steps from the Exchequer into Westminster, I followed two common jurymen, when I was a law officer of the crown, and I overheard one say to the other, 'I think we have given the crown verdicts enough: we may as well give them no more.'"

"Once," said he, "I had a very handsome offer made me. I was pleading for the rights of the inhabitants of the Isle of Man. Now, I had been reading in Coke, and I found there that the people of that island were no beggars. So, in my speech, I said, 'The people of the isle are no beggars; I therefore do not *beg* their rights—I *demand* them.' This so pleased an old smuggler who was present, that, when the trial was over, he called me aside and said, 'I'll tell you what, young gentleman; you shall have my daughter if you will marry her, and £100,000 for her fortune.' That was a very handsome offer; but I told him I had a wife who had nothing for her fortune, therefore I must stick to her."

When Chief-Justice of the Common Pleas, the following amusing case came before him at Exeter. He had to try a number of tailors, who were indicted before him for a riot arising out of a combination for a rise of wages. A witty barrister, who was retained for the defendants, cross-examining a witness as to the number present, his lordship reminded him, that as, according to law, "three may make a riot," the inquiry was irrelevant. "Yes, my lord," was the reply, "Hale and Hawkins lay down the law as your lordship states it, and I rely on their authority; for, if there must be *three men* to make a riot, the rioters being tailors, there must be nine times three present; and, unless the prosecutor makes out that there were twenty-seven joining in this breach of the peace, my clients are entitled to an acquittal." The Lord Chief-Justice (joining in the laugh) said, "Do you rely on common law or statute?"—"My lord, I rely on the well-known maxim, as old as Magna Charta, *Nine tailors make a man!*" Lord Eldon overruled the objection; but the jury took the law from the counsel instead of the judge, and acquitted all the defendants.

It is well known that Lord Eldon's dilatoriness and propensity to doubt were a constant subject of complaint and lamentation with the unfortunate suitors in Chancery. The following admirable *jeu d'esprit*, from the pen of Sir George Rose, professed to be a full record of all that occurred during one day's sitting of the court when his lordship presided:—

"Mr. Leach
Made a speech,
Impressive, clear, and strong;
Mr. Hart,
On the other part,
Was tedious, dull, and long.

> Mr. Parker
> Made that darker
> Which was dark enough without;
> Mr. Bell,
> He spoke so well,
> That the Chancellor said, 'I doubt!'"

This effusion, flying about Westminster Hall, reached the Chancellor, who was greatly amused by it, notwithstanding its allusion to his own great defect. Shortly after, Mr. Rose, having to argue a case before him, received from him the following well-turned retort: Giving his opinion with much gravity, he concluded thus—"For which reasons, the judgment must be against your clients; *and here, Mr. Rose, the Chancellor does not doubt.*"

Lord Eldon was fond of telling a story of a very old lady, a peeress, who came into court in person, when Lord Thurlow was Chancellor, to be examined touching her consent to the transfer of some property. This business being done, Lord Thurlow said he would not detain her. "But," said she, "I should be glad if your lordship would let me stay a little longer, for my cause has now been in court eighty-two years, and I want to know how they are going on about settling it." This anecdote served him very well when there were allusions made to the delays in Chancery in his own time.

His facetiousness was often embellished by the kind-heartedness and good humour which accompanied it. Once when travelling the circuit in company with a friend, who (according to a not uncommon usage in those days) carried pistols with him, which he placed beside his bed at night, they slept at a village inn, when, at dawn of day, Mr. Scott found in his chamber a figure dressed in black. Being sharply challenged, the intruder said, "I am only a poor sweep, sir, and I believe I have come down the wrong chimney."—"My friend," was his answer, you have come down the right; for I give you a sixpence to buy a pot of beer, and the gentleman in the next room sleeps with pistols at his pillow, and he would have blown your brains out had you paid him a visit."

It chanced, one day, as he was looking at his own picture in the Exhibition, two lively damsels placed themselves in front of him, and began to criticise it; one saying to the other, "I think, dear, we have seen enough of that stern-looking Chancellor, so let us go on." Whereupon he said, with a smile and his best bow, "And yet, young ladies, if you knew him, he would be happy to convince you that he is really a good-tempered old gentleman."

When in his eightieth year, he was still robust and hale enough to take exercise on foot; and being one day walking in St. James's Street, he fell in with a crowd gathered to see some passing cavalcade. Suddenly he felt a man's hand in one of his pockets; but as, luckily, it was not the one which contained his purse, he was content to laugh at the thief's disappointment; and quietly turning to him, said, "Ah, friend! you were wrong there: this other was the side where the *grab* lay!"

The Lord Chancellor, when in the country, amused himself with feeding his dogs and following the game, but, although he had all his life been fond of handling a gun, he was a wretched sportsman. As he wandered about the fields in a shabby jacket, with gaiters and a weather-beaten hat, his official dignity was little guessed at by strangers. In consequence he had several curious rencontres; one of which he thus related:—"I unfortunately crossed a lane in pursuit of my game, and in the second field from this lane I was accosted by a powerful and almost savage looking farmer, who challenged me as the poacher for whom he had long been in wait. I at once acknowledged that I might have made a mistake as to his land, and offered to turn back immediately, but this did not at all pacify him, for putting himself in front of me, he declared that I should not stir till he knew who I was and where to be found. I tried to evade giving a description of myself by renewed offers of departure and a promise not to return, but this did but increase his violence, and so I was at last forced to acknowledge that I was the Lord Chancellor,—a communication which was so far from allaying his ire that it did but increase its fury, for in language which looked very like earnest, he *swore* that, of all the impudent answers he ever got, mine was the most impudent, and I verily believe he would have laid hands on me if my tall footman (one of the finest young men I ever saw), had not come up to us and addressed me as, My lord."

In his own adopted county, Dorsetshire, he was regarded with great veneration, as the following ludicrous anecdote proves:—"When out shooting at Encombe (said he), we went through a field where a boy was employed to drive off the crows and the rooks from the new-sown wheat. I perceived the boy following us in our sport at least a mile from that field. 'My boy,' said I, 'how came you to leave your work? The birds will get all the wheat.' 'Oh, no, my lord,' said the boy (he must have been an own cousin of the "Artful Dodger"), 'they saw your lordship in the field, and they won't dare come again, now they know your lordship has been there.'"

He was rather a strict preserver of his game, though generally disposed to deal leniently with offenders in a personal encounter. One day he required a half-pay captain to show his certificate. "Who are you?" said the trespasser, "I suppose one of old Bags' keepers." "No," replied the Chancellor with a smile, "I am old Bags himself."

His conclusion of each sporting season at Encombe is said to have been a perfect jubilee for all his dogs. Pointers, spaniels, Newfoundlanders, terriers, &c., all, in short, of every kind and description, were turned out, and permitted to share in the fun. Their kind-hearted master took more pleasure in the enjoyment of these four-footed retainers, than in securing a large amount of game. It is said that one day, as he was preparing to leave the house for a day's sport, the gamekeeper ordered back some useless dogs of the pack, which forthwith uttered a whine of lamentation. Lord Eldon desired they should be allowed to accompany the party, and on the gamekeeper's remonstrating and saying they would probably destroy the sport, "Oh, never mind," was the answer, "let them go, poor things, 'tis a pity they should not have the enjoyment."

I shall conclude this chapter by quoting one more illustration of his kind-heartedness, united in this instance also with his characteristic love of fun. This was his answer to an application for a piece of preferment from his old friend Dr. Fisher, of the Charter House :—

"DEAR FISHER,—I cannot, to-day, give you the preferment for which you ask.

"I remain your sincere friend,

"ELDON.

"Turn over."

Then, on the other side,—

"I gave it you yesterday."

Referring to Lord Eldon's powers of conversation, Lord Brougham says :—"In relating anecdotes he excelled most men, and had an abundant store of them, though, of course, from the habit of his life they were chiefly professional, his application of them to passing events was singularly happy. The mingled grace and dignity of his demeanour added no small charm to his whole commerce with society, and, although the two brothers differed exceedingly in this respect, it was usual to observe that, except Sir W. Scott, no man was so agreeable as Lord Eldon."

XII.

Sir Samuel Romilly.

LORD BROUGHAM, in his "Sketches of Statesmen who Flourished in the Time of George III.," has given a most eloquent eloge of Sir S. Romilly. After dwelling with delight on the unsullied purity and elevated morality of his character, he pronounces him "a person of the most natural and simple manners, and one in whom the kindest charities and warmest feelings of human nature were blended in the largest measure with firmness of purpose and unrelaxed sincerity of principle." He goes on to say, further, that his capacity was of the highest order, and that the rare qualities he possessed, under the guidance of the most persevering industry, and with the stimulus of a lofty ambition, rendered him unquestionably the first advocate and the most profound lawyer of the age he flourished in, and placed him high among the ornaments of the senate. He adds, "As his practice, so his authority at the bar and with the bench was unexampled, and his success in Parliament was great and progressive."

After reading this eloquent eulogium, we eagerly inquire by what training did this admirable individual succeed in reaching so rare an excellence, and who were the great masters that taught him knowledge, directed him in the acquirement of his various information, and regulated the method of his self-culture? Happily he has given us a beautiful sketch of his early life, in which he satisfies our curiosity on these points to the utmost.

Sir S. Romilly was born in London, on the 1st March 1757. His grandfather, a French Protestant, was entitled by inheritance to a considerable landed estate at Montpellier, but, when about seventeen years old, he made a journey to Geneva, where he met with the celebrated Saurin, who happened to be on a visit there. So great was the impression left upon the mind of the youth by the conversation he had with this extraordinary man, that he came to a determination to abandon for ever his native country, his friends, and the inheritance that awaited him, and to trust to his own industry for a subsistence amidst strangers and in a foreign land, that he might enjoy the blessings of civil and religious liberty.

This purpose he carried into effect, and after a time succeeded in establishing himself in the business of a wax-bleacher, near London. He had a numerous family, and enjoyed a season of prosperity, but in the end experienced sad reverses of fortune. His father, who had assisted him with remittances, died, and a distant relation, being the next Catholic heir, succeeded to the family estate. Difficulties soon multiplied upon him, and bankruptcy and poverty were the consequences. Unable to endure these calamities, his spirit sank, and he died broken-hearted at the early age of forty-nine, leaving a widow with eight children.

The youngest of this orphan family was Peter, the father of Sir Samuel, who was brought up to the trade of a jeweller, in which he became successful and eminent. His illustrious son drew an attractive portrait of this worthy man :—

"He used often to talk to his children of the pleasure of doing good, and of the rewards which virtue found in itself; and from his lips that doctrine came to us, not as a dry and illusive precept, but as a heart-felt truth, and as the fruit of the happiest experience. All his amusements were such as his home only could afford him. He was fond of reading, and he had formed for himself a small, but a tolerably well-chosen library. He was an admirer of the fine arts, but pictures being too costly for his purchase, he limited himself to prints; and in the latter part of his life, as he grew richer, indulging himself in this innocent luxury to a degree perhaps of extravagance, he had at last a very large and valuable collection. He took pleasure in gardening, and he hired a small garden, in which he passed during the summer most of the few leisure hours his business afforded him.

"Naturally, my father was of the most cheerful disposition, always in good humour, always kind and indulgent, always even in the worst circumstances disposed to expect the best, enjoying all the good he met with in life, and consoling himself in adversity with the hope that it would not be of long duration." Having lost several children in infancy, Mr. Romilly, thinking the air of the town was unhealthy, hired some lodgings for his family at Marylebone, "then a small village, about a mile distant from town," and he had the happiness of succeeding in this experiment, for all the three children born afterwards lived to years of maturity. His mother's health being very ailing, little Samuel, with his brother and sister, were principally brought up by a kind and pious relative, Mrs. Margaret Facquier, who had lived in the family many years. When she was incapable of attending to her charge from sickness, they were intrusted to the care of a maid-servant, named Mary Evans, a kind-hearted, loving girl, who completely won the affections of the children, especially Samuel, who says of her: "She was to me in the place of a mother. I loved her to adoration. I remember when quite a child, unseen by her, kissing the clothes which she wore, and when she once entertained a design of quitting our family, going up into my room in an agony of affliction, and imploring God upon my knees to avert so great a calamity."

From his earliest infancy this gifted child was of a serious and somewhat melancholy disposition. He was also possessed of a lively imagination, easily alarmed by stories of witches and apparitions, and filled with terror by relations of murders and acts of cruelty. The prints which he found in the "Lives of the Martyrs" and the "Newgate Calendar" cost him many sleepless nights, and he was often so agitated with these impressions as to be equally afraid of remaining awake in the dark, and of falling asleep to encounter the terrors of his dreams.

This morbid sensitiveness took the shape of a constant dread lest his beloved father should be seized from him by death, and, if he were absent from home but an hour longer than usual, the little self-tormentor conjured up a thousand accidents, and when put to bed, lay sleepless and wretched until he heard the well-known knock at the hall door.

"My imagination," he says, "was the faculty which I most exercised, and it was often very busily employed when those about me were little aware of it. During the winter months we were always very regular on Sundays in our attendance at church. My father had a pew in one of the French chapels which had been established when the Protestant refugees first emigrated into England, and he required us to attend alternately there and at the parish church. It was a kind of homage to the faith of his ancestors, and it was a means of rendering the French language familiar to us; but nothing was ever worse calculated to inspire the mind of a child with respect for religion than such a kind of religious worship. . . . A large uncouth room, which presented to the view only irregular unpainted pews and dusty plastered walls; a congregation consisting principally of some strange-looking old women, scattered here and there; and a clergyman reading the service and preaching in a monotonous tone of voice and in a language not familiar to me, was not likely either to impress my mind with much religious awe, or to attract my attention to the doctrines which were delivered. In truth, I did not even attempt to attend to them; my mind was wandering to other subjects, and disporting itself in much gayer scenes than those before me, and little of religion was mixed in my reveries."

His education—"if, indeed," he says, "the little instruction I ever received from masters deserves to be so called"—was miserably defective. He was sent with his brother to a day school frequented by the children of the French refugees in London, the master of which was ignorant, and tyrannical, and incompetent to instruct his pupils in anything beyond reading, writing, and the elements of the French language. It had been Mr. Romilly's particular wish that his younger son should learn Latin, but, although it was professedly taught at the school, neither master nor ushers could construe a sentence of the easiest Latin prose; it is needless to say their pupils remained ignorant. The motive of the worthy jeweller in this wish had been his intention to bring up Samuel to the business of a solicitor. He accordingly endeavoured by his conversation to give the lad a favourable opinion of the way of life of a lawyer—"or rather of an attorney, for his ideas certainly soared no higher." But unfortunately for the success of his plan, the only attorney known to Mr. Romilly's family was by no means an attractive specimen of the genus. "He was a shortish fat man, with a ruddy countenance, which always shone as if besmeared with grease; a large wig, which sat loose from his head; his eyes constantly half shut and drowsy; all his motions slow and deliberate, and his words slabbered out as if he had not exertion enough to articulate. His dark and gloomy house was filled with dusty papers and voluminous parchment deeds; and in his meagre library I did not see a single volume which I should not have been deterred by its external appearance from opening. The idea of a lawyer and of Mr. L—— were so identified in my mind, that I looked upon the profession with disgust, and entreated my father to think of any way of life for me but that."

It was then proposed to place him in the commercial house of the Fludyers, who were near relations of his family, and one of whom, Sir Samuel Fludyer, was his godfather. With a view to this employment, he received instruction in book-keeping and mercantile accounts, but the death of both the partners in the house of Fludyer put an end to this promising project; and his father, having failed in several other schemes for his settlement, eventually employed him in his own trade, at first merely to give him employment, and afterwards with the intention that both brothers should succeed to his business, which, if skilfully managed, would afford an ample provision for them.

During the intervals of leisure which this new employment afforded him, the youth amused himself by reading indiscriminately all kinds of books which fell in his way. After a short experience he found his father's business not at all to his taste, and began to lament that he had not been educated for some literary profession. He considered that it was not yet too late for him, with an abundance of zeal, to make a very great progress; and when between fifteen and sixteen years of age, applied himself seriously to learn Latin, and having mastered the grammar, took daily an hour's lesson of a Scotchman named Paterson, who was a good scholar and carefully corrected the Latin exercises of his pupil. With this assistance, by means of hard study, he acquired considerable proficiency. He says, "In the course of three or four years during which I thus applied myself, I had read every prose writer of the ages of pure Latinity, except those who have treated merely of technical subjects, such as Varro, Columella, and Celsus. I had gone three times through the whole of Livy, Sallust, and Tacitus; I had read all Cicero (with two or three exceptions). I had studied the most celebrated of his orations, his Lœlius, his Cato Major, his treatise De

Oratore, and his Letters, and had translated a great part of them. Terence, Virgil, Horace, Ovid, and Juvenal I had read again and again. From Ovid and from Virgil I made many translations in verse. At the time, they appeared to me to have such merit, that I remember reading with triumph, first Dryden's translation and then my own, to my good-natured relations, who concurred with me in thinking that I had left poor Dryden at a most humiliating distance; a proof certainly, not of the merit of my verses, but of the badness of my judgment, the excess of my vanity, and the blind partiality of my friends."

He adds that he also attempted the study of Greek, but without success, and contented himself with studying the Greek authors by means of Latin versions. In addition to his classical studies he also read books of travel and history, and this always with maps before him, by which means he acquired a tolerable knowledge of geography. He also gave some attention to natural history, and attended private lectures on natural philosophy, and lectures on painting, architecture, and anatomy delivered at the Royal Academy.

"Such," he says, "were my pursuits and my amusements;" and by his perseverance and unaided efforts to refine his taste and store his mind with elegant and useful knowledge, he was gradually preparing himself for his future honourable and exalted career. About this time a series of happy events took place in the young man's family. His mother's health, as she advanced in years, greatly improved, and the family circle was enlarged and enlivened by the addition of two young girls, the daughters of Mr. Romilly's brother, and who had been left orphans by the sudden death of their parents within a few days of each other. The pecuniary means, too, of the household had been largely increased by considerable legacies, among them a bequest of £2000 to Samuel Romilly; a most seasonable and happy event for him, as it enabled him to gratify his wish and to adopt a profession in accordance with his aspirations.

All these important occurrences came like sunshine to cheer the spirit and animate the hopes of the future Solicitor-General. His description of the domestic ménage is charming: "Upon receiving so large an accession to his fortune my father removed out of his country lodgings into a house still, however, at Marylebone. There our whole family now resided throughout the year, what had been our town house being appropriated entirely to business. Our new house was in High Street, and, to judge from its external appearance, its narrow form, its two small windows on a floor, and the little square piece of ground behind it, which was dignified with the name of a garden, one would have supposed that very scanty and very homely indeed must have been this our comparative opulence and luxury. But those who had mingled in our family, and had hearts to feel in what real happiness consists, would have formed a very different judgment. They would have found a lively, youthful, and accomplished society, blest with every enjoyment that an endearing home can afford; a society united by a similarity of tastes, dispositions, and affections, as well as by the strongest ties of blood. They would have admired our lively, varied, and innocent pleasures; our summer rides and walks in the cheerful country, which was close to us; our winter evening occupations of drawing, while one of us read aloud some interesting book, or the eldest of my cousins played and sang to us with exquisite taste and expression; the little banquets with which we celebrated the anniversary of my father's wedding, and of the birth of every member of our happy society; and the dances with which, in spite of the smallness of our rooms, we were frequently indulged.

"I cannot recollect the days, happily I may say the years, which thus passed away, without the most lively emotion. I love to transport myself in idea into our little parlour with its green paper, and the beautiful prints of Vivares, Bartolozzi, and Strange, from the pictures of Claude, Caracci, Raphael, and Correggio with which its walls were elegantly adorned; and to call again to mind the familiar and affectionate society of young and old intermixed, which was gathered round the fire; and even the Italian greyhound, the cat, and the spaniel, which lay in perfect harmony, basking before it. I delight to see the door open that I may recognise the friendly countenances of the servants, and, above all, of the old nurse, to whom we were all endeared, because it was while she attended my mother that her health had so much improved."

It is distressing to learn that, with such means of happiness and in the midst of enjoyments so well suited to his temper and disposition, this amiable being was not completely happy. The melancholy to which he had from childhood been subject, at intervals oppressed him; and his enjoyment was often poisoned by the reflection that at some time or other it must end. There can be no question these anxious feelings were the effect of disease, and it is deeply painful to reflect that he eventually fell a victim to a paroxysm of this congenital malady.

In the meantime, the dislike which young Romilly conceived for his father's business increasing every day, he earnestly longed for some other employment. His indulgent father readily listened to his wishes, and it was determined, after consultation with friends, that he should be articled for five years to one of the sworn clerks in Chancery. The mechanical duties of this office, though in some degree enlivened by his master's practice as a solicitor, were scarcely more attractive to him than his attendance upon his father's business. He found no amusement, and took but little interest in them; but they left him a great deal of leisure, which he turned to the best possible account. "I had soon laid out," he says, "the plan of my future life; which was to follow my profession just as far as was necessary for my subsistence, and to aspire to fame by my literary pursuits." With this object he resumed his studies with the utmost diligence, particularly devoting himself to strenuous exercise in prose composition; and also reading and studying the best English writers, noting with critical accuracy their modes of expression.

While thus engaged, he formed an acquaintance which had no small influence upon all the subsequent events of his life. It was that of Mr. John Roget, a clergyman and a native of Geneva, who had been chosen minister of the French chapel at which the Romillys attended. Of this gentleman, who afterwards became his brother-in-law, he speaks with ardent praise, describing his official services as marked by taste and eloquence, and himself as possessed of an ardent mind, a rich imagination, and exquisite sensibility. Immediately upon his arrival in England he became intimate with the family of Mr. Romilly, and greatly attached himself to Samuel, with whom he conversed about his studies, encouraging him to persevere in them, and often pronouncing the most favourable predictions as to his success in the attainment of superior excellence, and his rise in the profession he had chosen.

Sir S. Romilly's narrative is divided into two parts. The former was written when he had just attained his twenty-first year, and when his prospects were uncertain and his fortune yet to be made. He resumed his story when he had reached his fifty-sixth year. He was then the object of public attention, had attained to the highest rank in his profession, had filled the office of Solicitor-General, been knighted, and long occupied a place in the highest council of the realm, deservedly beloved and honoured as a public benefactor, by whose wise and philanthropic counsels the best interests of his countrymen were largely promoted.

During fifteen years he had tasted the choicest blessings of domestic life, and it was indeed for the sake of his children he was induced to resume the narrative of his early days. After a short introduction he thus continues his autobiography:—

"I had completed my twenty-first year before my resolution was taken, as to the course I should adopt. The encouragement I had received from Roget had inclined me, not only to continue in my profession, but to look up to a superior rank in it, and I accordingly determined, at this late period of life, to qualify myself for the bar, and entered myself of the Society of Gray's Inn, took there a very pleasant set of chambers, which overlooked the gardens; arranged my little collection of books about me, and began with great ardour the painful study of the law."

He was principally influenced in adopting this decision by a dislike to embarrass his father by withdrawing from his hands the bequest before alluded to, a step which would have been necessary had he carried out his original intention of purchasing a seat in the Six Clerks' Office, at the expiration of his articles. "At a later season of my life," he writes, "after a success at the bar which my wildest and most sanguine dreams had never painted to me, when I was gaining an income of £8,000 or £9,000 a year, I have often reflected how all that prosperity had arisen out of the pecuniary difficulties and confined circumstances of my father. There was another circumstance, which, though a trifling one, I ought to mention, for it certainly had some influence over the judgment which I exercised. The works of Thomas had fallen into my hands; I had read with admiration his Eloge of Daguesseau; and the career of glory which he represents that illustrious magistrate to have run, had excited to a very great degree my ardour and my ambition, and opened to my imagination new paths of glory."

He was now advised to become the pupil of some Chancery draftsman for a couple of years, and for the first year to confine himself merely to reading under his direction and with his assistance. This plan he pursued with great advantage, forming a common-place book as he read, which he found of the greatest use, indeed, indispensable to the profitable study of law reports. Nor did he confine himself to law alone, but still pursued his literary exercises, translating and composing, endeavouring to form for himself an elegant and correct style, employing much of his time in translating the Latin historians and orators, occasionally writing political essays for the newspapers (which he was much gratified to find were always inserted), and sometimes attending the houses of Parliament, exercising his powers by making imaginary answers to the speeches which he heard there.

The close application with which he pursued these studies before long proved injurious to his health, and in the spring of 1780 he went to drink the waters at Bath, but did not experience much benefit. In the beginning of June in that year broke out that extraordinary insurrection excited by Lord George Gordon, which, says Sir S. Romilly, has hardly any parallel in our history. "In a moment of profound peace and of perfect security the metropolis found itself on a sudden abandoned, as it were, to the plunder and the fury of a bigoted and frantic populace. One night, the flames were seen ascending from nine or ten different conflagrations, kindled by these unresisted insurgents. The Inns of Court were marked out as objects of destruction, and Gray's Inn, in which many Catholics resided, was particularly obnoxious. The barristers and students of the different Inns of Court determined to arm themselves in their own defence; I did as others did, was up a whole night under arms, and stood as sentinel for several hours at the gate in Holborn."

This fatigue and the excessive heat of the weather greatly aggravated his malady, and throughout the whole of the following winter he was a confirmed invalid. The following spring saw him no better, and he became possessed with the idea that his health was irrevocably lost, that he should be a wretched valetudinarian for the rest of his days, and that all his bright hopes for the future were at an end.

Fortunately he was induced to try the effect of a journey to Switzerland, and a visit to his sister and brother-in-law, M. Roget, who had taken up their residence at Geneva, and the change of scene, with the novelty and entertainments of the journey, and the congenial society of his relatives, soon dissipated his melancholy and gradually improved his health. Returning by way of Paris, he became acquainted in that capital with a great variety of persons—artists, advocates, and authors; amongst these were d'Alembert and Diderot, the most celebrated authors then remaining in France; and the conversation and correspondence of these and other eminent personages produced no small effect upon his subsequent opinions and character.

In Easter term, 1783, Mr. Romilly was called to the bar, but his entrance upon the business of the profession was delayed for some months in consequence of a second journey he took to Switzerland for the purpose of attending his sister to England on the death of M. Roget. The first long vacation was passed in the performance of this melancholy duty. By Michaelmas term, he says, "I had returned to business; or rather to attend the courts, and receive such business as accident might throw in my way. I had endeavoured to draw Chancery pleadings before I was called to the bar; in that way, however, the occupation I got under the bar was very inconsiderable; but soon after I was admitted I was employed to draw pleadings in several cases. This species of employment went on very gradually increasing for several years, during which, though I was occupied in the way of my profession, I had scarcely any occasion to open my lips in court.

"In the spring of 1784 I first went upon the circuit. All circuits were indifferent to me, for I had no friends or connections on any one of them; and my choice fell on the Midland, because there appeared to be fewer men of considerable talents or of high character as advocates upon it than upon any other, and consequently a greater opening for me than elsewhere; it was besides shorter than some other circuits, and what was no unimportant consideration, my travelling expenses upon it would be less."

A most amiable trait of his character is shown in the following incident. When he was called to the bar, it became necessary that he should have a servant to be always in chambers to receive briefs, &c., and to attend him upon the circuit in the various characters of clerk, valet, and groom. He chose, to fill this office, a poor infirm creature named Bickers, for no other reason than that he might show kindness to his old servant, Mary Evans—the much-loved attendant of his childhood. She had married this man, and they had fallen into poverty. Not having the means to provide for them in any other way, Mr. Romilly adopted this method. But, "I certainly suffered," he says, "during several years for my good nature. He could ride, and stand behind my chair at dinner; but this was almost all he could do; and though I sometimes employed him to copy papers for me, he wrote very ill and made a thousand faults of spelling." But this was not the worst of the thing. The man was a Methodist, and his appearance was singular and puritanical, affording an admirable butt for the ridicule of the young barristers who went the circuit, and who, on the first day of his appearance, bestowed on him the sobriquet of "the Quaker." To his other defects, he added a disposition occasionally to indulge in drinking, and at such times his young patron was under the constant apprehension he should say or do something which would afford an inexhaustible fund of mirth to the whole circuit.

Yet all this did the kind-hearted youth patiently endure for the sake of doing good, and he actually retained the man in his service till the day of his death—a period of some years. Bickers was not ungrateful. He was anxious to prove his zeal and attachment for his benefactor, and he took a curious method of showing his good will. "I shall not soon forget," says Sir Samuel, "the earnestness with which he once ventured to offer me his advice on a matter he judged to be of great importance. I had sometimes employed him to copy papers which I had amused myself with writing upon abuses existing in the administration of justice, and upon the necessity of certain reforms. He had seen with great regret the little progress I had made in my profession, and particularly upon the circuit, and had observed those whom he thought much my inferiors in talents, far before me in business, and putting these matters together in his head, he entertained no doubt that he had at last discovered the cause of what had long puzzled him. The business of a lawyer depends upon the good opinion of attorneys; and attorneys never could think well of any man who was troubling his head about reforming abuses, when he ought to be profiting by them! All this he one day took the liberty of representing to me with very great humility. I endeavoured to calm his apprehensions, and told him what I wrote was only seen by himself and by me, but this, doubtless, did not satisfy him."

In the year after that in which he was called to the bar Mr. Romilly first formed the acquaintance of the Count de Mirabeau, who was then in England. For this introduction he was indebted to his Parisian friends, and in a short time he became very intimate with this extraordinary man, in whose society he found a rich treat. He had not then attained to the great celebrity he afterwards acquired, but "as he had read much, had seen a great deal of the world, was acquainted with all the most distinguished persons who adorned either the royal court or the republic of letters in France, had a great knowledge of French and Italian literature, and possessed a very good taste, his conversation was extremely interesting and not a little instructive.

By Mirabeau he was introduced to Benjamin Vaughan, who made him acquainted with Lord Lansdowne, at the request of that nobleman, who upon learning that he was the author of an anonymous tract entitled "A Fragment on the Constitutional Power and Duties of Juries," had become desirous of his acquaintance, and begged that Mr. Romilly would call on him, in compliance with which desire the meeting took place. "He received me," says the autobiography, "in the most flattering manner. From that time he anxiously cultivated my acquaintance and my friendship; and to that friendship I owe it that I ever knew the affectionate wife who has been the author of all my happiness."

Lord Lansdowne's estimate of his character, and his high anticipation of his eventual success, are evinced by the fact that, in the first years of their acquaintance, and before Mr. Romilly's professional fortunes had begun to flow, he was twice offered a seat in Parliament by that nobleman, which he declined from a feeling of independence.

Lord Lansdowne was very desirous that his young friend should distinguish himself in his profession, and urged him to write some work which might bring him into notice. He especially directed his attention to a tract then recently published, and which excited at the time much attention,—Madan's "Thoughts on Executive Justice." This pamphlet was said to have had considerable influence with the judges in enforcing capital punishments. Being thus induced to examine the book, he represents himself as so much shocked by the folly and inhumanity of it, that, instead of enforcing the same arguments, he sat down to refute them, and shortly after produced a tractate entitled, "Strictures upon the Thoughts," accompanied by a letter of Dr. Franklin's upon the same subject. Thus was he first induced to consider with attention the principles of Criminal Law, to which, at a later period, he devoted himself with distinguished ability, energy, and perseverance, labouring in each successive session to procure the repeal of those harsh and terrible laws which were a disgrace to our statute books. He observes, "The little success of this pamphlet (of which not more than a hundred copies were sold) did not deter me from occupying my leisure hours in writing observations on different parts of our criminal law. Upon the circuit, too, I made the criminal law very much my study and attended as much as I could to the Crown Court, and noted down all the most remarkable things that passed there, not merely the points of law that arose, but the effects which the different provisions of the law, the rules of evidence, and our forms of proceeding appeared to me to produce on the manners of the people, and on the administration of justice."

For these studies he had, unfortunately, ample leisure. At the end of his sixth or seventh circuit he had made no progress, and this might have continued to be the case had he not adopted a measure which he heard Mr. Justice Heath strongly recommend: he said, "There was no use in going a circuit without attending sessions." This experiment proved very successful in the case of Mr. Romilly; and he had not attended many sessions before he was in all the business there. This naturally led to business at the assizes, and he tells us that he had obtained a larger portion of it than any man upon the circuit before his occupation in London compelled him to relinquish it altogether.

In the vacation of the year 1788 Mr. Romilly made another visit to Paris, where he saw all the notabilities of the day and renewed his acquaintance with Mirabeau. It is interesting to read the following observations made by so intelligent an observer on the eve of the great French Revolution:—

"The state of public affairs during this visit was highly

interesting. The administration of the Archbishop of Sens had become extremely unpopular, and there were some trifling commotions in the streets. Crowds assembled on the Pont Neuf, and obliged all the passers-by to take off their hats in token of respect, before the equestrian statue of Henry IV. In the coffee-houses of the Palais Royal the freest conversations were indulged, and in the midst of the public ferment which prevailed a change of ministry was announced, and M. Necker was recalled to the administration. He had not long returned to office before the king declared his determination to assemble the States General. Such an event, as may well be supposed, produced a very great effect, and was the subject of every conversation. The best and most virtuous men saw in it the beginning of a new era of happiness for France, and for all the civilized world. . . . . There was not, however, to be found a single individual, the most gloomy, the most timid, or the most enthusiastically sanguine who foresaw any of the extraordinary events to which the assembling the States was to lead. Who indeed could, in that single measure, have discovered the seeds of what followed?—the abolition of the monarchy; the public execution of the king and queen; the destruction of the nobility; the annihilation of all religion; the erection of a petty but most sanguinary tyranny in almost every town of France; a succession of wars; all contributing to increase the martial glory of the nation; and, finally, the establishment of a military despotism, the subjugation of almost all the rest of Europe, and the nearest approach that is to be found in the history of modern times to universal empire?"

He was himself among those who, in the early stages

of the French Revolution, entertained the most sanguine expectations of the happy effects which were to result from it, not to France alone, but to the rest of the world, and in 1790 he published a short pamphlet on the subject, entitled, "Thoughts on the Probable Influence of the French Revolution on Great Britain;" but a subsequent visit to Paris, just on the eve of the insurrection which ended in bringing the royal family to Paris, served to give him a much less favourable opinion of the state of affairs than he had previously entertained.

At this point in his history the narrative closes. I shall conclude this chapter with an extract from a letter written by him the year before his lamented decease, at a time when it was supposed that he aspired to the office of Lord Chancellor:—"Already I have attained the very summit of my wishes. The happiness of my present condition cannot be increased: it may be essentially impaired. I am at the present moment completely independent both of the favours and of the frowns of Government. The large income which I enjoy and which is equal to all my wishes, has been entirely produced by my own industry and exertion; for no portion of it am I indebted to the Crown; of no particle of it is it in the power of the Crown to deprive me. The labours of my profession, great as they are, yet leave me some leisure both for domestic, and even for literary enjoyments. In those enjoyments, in the retirement of my study, in the bosom of my family, in the affection of my relations, in the kindness of my friends, in the good-will of my fellow-citizens, in the uncourted popularity which I know that I enjoy, I find all the good that human life can supply."

XIII.

Lord Tenterden.

"LABORE."

FIRST BEGINNINGS.

LET me advise the thoughtful reader to spell over and over again the single word that stands at the head of this chapter. It is the motto which Lord Tenterden selected on his promotion to the Bench, as indicative of the cause of his success in life.

And, true indeed it is, that, without steady application, whatever may be a man's abilities, he cannot expect to make a lawyer of distinction, nor will he ever write his own passport to rank and fortune.

I feel it is a pleasant task to trace the upward progress of this excellent individual; a man of very obscure origin, and by no means naturally gifted with brilliant abilities; but who, by dint of industry, self-denial, and unsullied integrity, won for himself the esteem of his contemporaries, and will ever be respected as a great magistrate and a man of true worth.

Charles Abbott was born in Canterbury on the 7th October, 1762; his father, who followed the trade of a barber, lived at the corner of a narrow street, opposite the stately western portal of the cathedral. There, in a small, mean-looking house, the future Chief-Justice of England first saw the light, being the youngest child of his parents, a respectable and hardworking couple. The father was described by one who knew him well, as "a tall, erect, primitive-looking man, with a large pig-tail, which, latterly assumed the aspect of a heavy brass knocker of a door." The mother was a devout, praise-worthy woman, and both struggled meritoriously to bring up their children in habits of honest industry. Little did they imagine their domestic cares should one day be rewarded by a son who would rise to distinction, and with loving remembrance record their merits upon his tomb, in the following line:—

"Patre vero prudenti, matre piâ ortus."

Having learned to read at a dame's school, the child took to accompanying his father, on his daily rounds, and we have a graphic picture of the old man "going about with the instruments of his business under his arms, and attended frequently by his son Charles, a youth as decent, grave, and primitive-looking as himself." There seemed every likelihood that the boy would, in due time, step into his father's shoes, and run a course as obscure, but happily for him the excellent grammar-school of his native city offered to humble day-scholars the means of a sound education at small expense. Thither he was sent, at the age of seven years, being admitted on the foundation of the King's School, established by Henry VIII., and then under the tuition of Dr. Osmund Beauvoir, an admirable classical scholar, and a man of refined taste and discrimination.

There he had for school-fellow, the well-known literary baronet Sir Egerton Brydges, who was through life his attached and steadfast friend, and who has given a pleasing account of him in his boyish days:—

"From his earliest years he was industrious, apprehensive, regular, and correct in all his conduct—even in his temper, and prudent in everything. I became acquainted with him in July, 1775, when I was removed from Maidstone to Canterbury school. I was nearly his age, and was placed in the same class with him, in which I won the next place to him, and kept it, till I quitted school for Cambridge, in 1780.

"Though we were in some degree competitors, oui friendship was never broken or cooled. He always exceeded me in accuracy, steadiness, and equality of labour; he knew the rules of grammar better, and was more sure in any examination or task. He wrote Latin verses and prose themes with more correctness, and in temper was always prudent and calm. Each knew well where the other's strength lay, and yielded to it."

Another schoolfellow of the patient, industrious Abbott, who himself rose to high preferment in the church, adds,—"I remember him well; grave, silent, and demure, always studious and well-behaved; reading his book, instead of accompanying us to play, and recommending himself to all who saw and knew him by his quiet and decent demeanour. The clergy of Canterbury always took great notice of him, as they knew and respected his father. . . . . When Lord Tenterden and Mr. Justice Richards, on going the circuit, once visited the cathedral of Canterbury, the latter took notice of a singing man in the choir who had an excellent voice. 'Ay, brother,' said Lord Tenterden, 'that is the only man I ever envied; when at school in this town, we were candidates together for a chorister's place, and he obtained it.'"

Subsequent events proved that this was a most fortunate disappointment for the future Chief-Justice, who, like a sensible lad, instead of yielding to discouragement, applied with increased diligence to his studies, and in this manner secured the regard of his master, and in due time rose to the captaincy of the school. At the age of seventeen it became necessary that he should determine on his future course in life. There seemed no alternative but for him to drudge at his father's trade, since he had not the means of completing his education, and thus fitting himself for a liberal profession. There was, however, a general wish that his industry and abilities should be rewarded, and by the aid of private generosity his outfit was quickly provided, and the trustees of the school conferred on him a small exhibition in their gift, afterwards adding a pittance from the funds of the establishment sufficient, with rigorous economy, to support him until he should have obtained his B.A. degree.

He was accordingly entered as a member of Corpus Christi College, Oxford, in the spring of the year 1781, about six years after Lord Eldon and his brother Lord Stowell had become members of University College. Thus, at the same time, there were three men at the university (one of them a scholar holding an exhibition not exceeding sixteen pounds per annum; the two others, holding fellowships, not exceeding one hundred and twenty pounds annually), who were destined to become the three heads of the Law—the one as Lord Chancellor, the second as Lord Chief-Justice, and the third, as judge of the Admiralty and Prerogative Courts. Perhaps there were not at the time three more simple, humble, modest-looking men within the precincts of the university, and certainly not three men from whose precedents and deportment any one would less have augured so splendid a future.*

We have an interesting account of the young gownsman's first entrance upon college life. Immediately after his arrival at Oxford he became candidate for a vacant scholarship, and thus described his feelings on the occasion in a letter to his *fides Achates;* who was then just entered at Queen's College, Cambridge :—

"*March* 18, 1781.

"DEAR EGERTON,—I have been a week in Oxford, and almost finished the examination; the day of election is next Tuesday. I cannot look forward without great dread, for my expectations of success are by no means sanguine. . . . . As yet I have kept to my resolution of drinking nothing. How long further I shall, I know not, but I hope my pride will soon serve to strengthen it. I wish Tuesday were over."

"*Monday Night.*

"This has been a heavy day indeed. I would not pass another in such anxiety for two scholarships. Disappointment would be easier borne than such a doubtful situation. It is a great pleasure to me to be able to reflect that there is one person who will feel for me. What happiness would it have been to me had we had the good fortune to be both of the same university. Our examination has been very strict. . . . . Good-night."

* See *Gentleman's Magazine* for 1832.

"*Tuesday*, 12 *o'clock.*

"At last it is all over, and—now your expectations are at the highest—I am—guess—elected. You will see, from my manner of writing that I am very much pleased, and so, in truth, I am. The president said to me (but don't mention it to any one), that I had gained it entirely by my merit—that I had made a very good appearance, and so had all the other candidates,—Yours most affectionnately, C. ABBOTT."

This agitated epistle, written in the midst of suspense and excitement was followed by one which cannot fail to enlist our sympathies cordially on his behalf:—

"C. C. C., *April* 3, 1781.

"Yes, my dear Egerton, it does give me the most heartfelt pleasure to hear how kindly my friends rejoice in my success. Believe me, the chief pleasure that I feel on this occasion is reading my letters of congratulation. I needed nothing to assure me of your friendship. Had any proof been wanting, your kind letter would have been sufficient. The examination was indeed a tedious piece of work, but I would go through twice the trouble for the pleasure of knowing that I had answered the expectation of my friends.

"I have received two letters from my dearest mother, in which she gives me an account how sincerely all my friends at Canterbury have congratulated her on my success—and friends so much superior to our humble condition, that she says, 'such a universal joy as appeared on the occasion I believe hardly ever happened in a town left by a tradesman's son.' Who would not undergo any labour to give pleasure to such parents? . . . .

You have heard me wish that I had never been intended for the university. It was impious; it was ungrateful. I banish the thought for ever from my heart. Not that I foresee much pleasure in a college life; but I know that my present situation is perhaps the only comfort to those whose age and misfortunes have rendered some alleviation of care absolutely necessary. Pardon the expression of these sentiments to you, and consider that they flow from the breast of a son.

"What a dissatisfied wretch I am! But a little while past to be a scholar of Corpus was the height of my ambition; that summit is (thank heaven) gained;—when another and another appears still in view. In a word, I shall not rest easy till I have ascended the rostrum in the theatre."

His biographers mention with praise the exemplary conduct of the youth during the whole of his academical career. With strict economy and care he was able to preserve a decent appearance, and giving his undivided attention to the object he had in view, was preserved from those temptations which idleness and luxurious habits present to the unwary "freshmen," so many of whom fall victims to such snares. Instead of incurring debts by giving wine-parties and buying hunters, he, from the first hour of his college career, resolutely abstained from all self-indulgence, and on the authority of Lord Campbell it is stated as a curious fact that he never, in the whole course of his life, mounted on horseback. This he related, in his latter years, to an old friend who recommended him to try horse-exercise. He said, "he should be sure to fall off, like an ill-balanced sack of corn, as he had never crossed a horse any more than a rhinoceros, and had now become too stiff and feeble to begin a course of cavaliering."

At the time when Abbott ran his college career, there was no opportunity of shining as "first wrangler;" and the only academical honours that could be gained were chancellor's medals for Latin and English composition, both which he eventually carried off. His first attempt was unsuccessful, but in the following year he was more fortunate. The subject of his prize poem was "Globus Ærostaticus;" the wonders of Lunardi's air-balloon having filled the minds of men with amazement and speculation. "I have often," says Lord Campbell in his "Lives of the Chancellors," "I have often heard my father relate the consternation excited by this same Lunardi in the county of Fife. He had ascended from Edinburgh, and the wind carried him across the Frith of Forth. The inhabitants of Cupar had observed a speck, which was at first supposed to be a bird, grow into a large globe, and pass at no great height over their heads, with a man in a boat depending from it. Some thought they could descry about him the wings of an angel, and believed that the day of judgment had arrived." Apparently inspired with enthusiasm by this novel theme, the young orator, as victor, mounted the rostrum, and amidst loud plaudits, recited his beautiful lines, numbering one hundred and fifty-eight. He thus announced his success to his friend Egerton:—

"C. C. C., *June* 16, 1784.

"I have delayed writing to you for some time, partly because I waited for the decision of the prizes, but principally because I have been constantly employed in endeavouring to escape my own thoughts by company and every means I could. I am now, however, repaid for my anxieties. They say it was a hard run thing. There were sixteen compositions sent in. . . . . All that has happened since this morning appears a dream."

Not long after, this dutiful son had to lament the death of his excellent father. His poor widowed mother became now the object of his affectionate concern, and for her sake he declined an advantageous offer to go to Virginia as tutor to a young man of very large fortune there. He was willing to forego a considerable part of his own salary, so that £50 a year might be settled upon her for life. "This," he wrote to his friend, "with the little left her by my father, would afford her a comfortable subsistence without the fatigue of business, which she is becoming very unable to bear." But this condition was declined, and consequently the matter dropped.

The following year found him again a successful candidate for the English Essay. The subject was, *The Use and Abuse of Satire.* In this composition he displayed "nice critical discrimination, and exquisite good sense," and showed he had already acquired that superior English style which afterwards distinguished his celebrated book on the *Law of Ships*, and his written judgments when Chief-Justice of the King's Bench.

These hardly-won honours secured for Mr. Abbott the general admiration of his compeers, and he was soon rewarded with a college fellowship and appointed junior tutor with Mr. Burgess (afterwards the Bishop of Salisbury), who entertained a warm regard for him, and in after life used often to mention his early history as remarkably illustrative of the intimate connection between studious and moral habits, and future professional success.

In addition to this engagement he took private pupils in classics, and became tutor to Mr. Yarde, the son of Mr. Justice Buller, at a salary of a hundred guineas per annum. This introduction proved in the end very advantageous for him, as it brought him under the notice of that learned and sagacious judge, who immediately perceived and appreciated his solid and useful talents, and recommended him to embrace the profession of the law, rather than that of the church, to which he had hitherto inclined. This may be regarded as the turning-point of his history, for he was induced to follow the sage counsel of his new friend, and to submit to the sacrifices and incur the risks necessarily attending this change of purpose.

He was then in his twenty-sixth year, and had resided seven years in his college. Henceforward he devoted his whole attention to preparation for his new pursuit, and on the 16th November 1787, was admitted a student of the Middle Temple, and soon afterwards hired a small set of chambers in Brick Court. We may imagine him patiently submitting to all the drudgery of attendance at Attorney's offices, and pupilage under the celebrated George Wood, the great master of Special Pleading. Nothing could exceed his industry, and there seemed to be a natural adaptation in his mind for the acquirement of the mysteries of this peculiar science, insomuch that "he is supposed to have more rapidly qualified himself for its practice than any man before or since." By-and-by he commenced business, as a pleader under the bar, and by diligence, despatch, and reasonable terms secured clients in greater numbers than he had hoped for, and no client that once entered his chambers ever forsook him. During seven years he continued after this fashion steadily advancing in the regard of his associates, and securing, by his pupils and his business, an income sufficiently large to venture upon an early marriage.

On the 30th July, 1795, he wedded Mary, daughter of Mr. Lamotte, a gentleman of fortune, residing at Basilden, in Kent, to whom he had been for some time attached. The father of the lady is said to have called at the chambers of the young lawyer, and upon asking him "what means he had to maintain a wife?" received this pithy answer, "The books in this room, and two pupils in the next."

To such good account did he turn these resources that in a short time his professional gains amounted to some thousands a year. During each succeeding year his income continued to increase, and, at the time of his death, the thrifty lawyer was in possession of a large real estate, and of personal property to the amount of £120,000.

There is not much of stirring interest in the subsequent course of Mr. Abbott; and instead of tracing his history step by step, it may be preferable to relate a few characteristic traits of his official and personal character.

His legal abilities ranked very high in the opinion of the men best qualified to judge,—those who were themselves skilled in the science of the law, and in the practice of the courts. Lord Brougham has drawn a portrait of him which is not only full of wise discrimination, but most instructive in the lessons it conveys to all who aspire to tread in such high places, and for whom the virtues of self-control and impartiality are pre-eminently requisite. He says:—

"A man of great legal abilities and of a reputation, though high, by no means beyond his merits. On the contrary it may be doubted if he ever enjoyed all the fame that his capacity and his learning entitled him to. . . . . Although his reputation at the bar was firmly established for a long course of years, it was not till he became a judge, hardly till he became Chief-Justice, that his merits were fully known. It then appeared that he had a singularly judicial understanding, and even the defects which had kept him in the less ambitious walks of the profession—his caution, his aversion to all that was experimental, his want of fancy—contributed, with his greater qualities, to give him a very prominent rank indeed among our ablest judges.

One defect alone he had, which was likely to impede his progress towards this eminent station; but of that he was so conscious as to protect himself against it by constant and effectual precautions. His temper was naturally bad; it was hasty and it was violent; forming a marked contrast with the rest of his mind. But it was singular with what success he fought against this, and how he mastered the rebellious part of his nature. Indeed it was a study to observe this battle, or rather victory, for the conflict was too successful to be apparent on many occasions. On the bench it rarely broke out, but there was observed a truly praiseworthy feature, singularly becoming in the demeanour of a judge. Whatever struggles there might be carried on with the advocate during the heat of a cause, and how great soever might be the asperity shown on either part, all passed away—all was, even to the vestige of the trace of it, discharged from his mind, when the peculiar duty of the judge came to be performed; and he directed the jury in every particular, as if no irritation had ever passed over his mind in the course of the cause. . . . .

"Whoever has practised at Nisi Prius, knows well how rare it is to find a judge of an unquiet temper, especially one of an irascible disposition, who can go through the trial without suffering his course to be affected by the personal conflicts which may have taken place in the course of it. It was, therefore, an edifying sight to observe Lord Tenterden, whose temper had been visibly affected during the trial (for on the bench he had not always the entire command of it, which we have described him as possessing while at the bar), addressing himself to the points in the cause, with the same perfect calmness and indifference with which a mathematician pursues the investigation of an abstract truth, as if there were neither the parties nor the advocates in existence, and only bent upon the discovering and the elucidation of truth."

Some rather amusing tales are told of Lord Tenterden's occasional impatience and causticity by Mr. Townsend, in his "Lives of the Judges." In his eagerness to cut off all the fringes of rhetoric and to compel despatch he would break in upon the discussions of the long-robed gentlemen in a manner the reverse of courteous.

Thus, one day in banco, a learned counsel, who had lectured on the law, and was much addicted to oratory, came to argue a special demurrer. "My client's opponent," he commenced, "worked like a mole underground, *clam et secreté;*" to this no response came but an indignant grunt from the Chief-Justice. "It is asserted in Aristotle's Rhetoric." "I dont want to hear what is asserted in Aristotle's Rhetoric," interposed Lord Tenterden. The advocate shifted his ground and took up, as he thought, a safe position. "It is laid down in the Pandects of Justinian." "Where are you got to now?" "It is a principle of the civil law." "Oh, sir!" exclaimed the judge, with a tone and voice which abundantly justified his assertion, "we have nothing to do with the civil law in this court."

At another time Mr. Brougham opened an action for the amount of a wager laid upon a dog fight, which, through some unwillingness of dogs or men, had not been brought to an issue: "We, my Lord," said the advocate, "were minded that the dogs should fight." "Then I," replied the Judge, "am minded to hear no more of it! Call the next cause."

Correct, appropriate, and succinct in his own statements, he could not endure conceit or affectation in the language of others. He was irate if a *shop* were called a *warehouse*, or a *shopman* dubbed himself *assistant.* A gentleman pressing into a crowded court complained that he could not get to his counsel. "What are you, sir?" asked the Judge. "My Lord, I am the plantiff's solicitor." "We know nothing of solicitors here, sir, had you been in the respectable rank of an *attorney* I should have ordered room to be made for you." A country apothecary, in answer to some plain questions using very unnecessarily high-sounding medical phraseology, the Chief-Justice roared out, "Speak English, sir, if you can; or I must swear an interpreter."

What our judge best loved was a direct reply, and he was for keeping himself and everybody else to the precise matter in hand. Latterly, when oppressed with labour and disease, his formerly handsome and impressive features assumed an aspect of settled severity. "Sallow and care-worn, they seemed to borrow the expression of the lion in the royal arms on the tapestry behind him, while with determination he frowned down any attempt to raise useless quibbles, and harshly stopped all unnecessary speech." *

Although it was supposed he rather shrank from any allusion to his obscure origin and boyish days, unless in the company of intimate friends, he was once complimented upon his rise under circumstances so extravagantly ludicrous, that he joined in the general shout of laughter the orator called forth. Sir Peter Laurie, the saddler, when Lord Mayor of London, gave a dinner at the Mansion House to the judges, and, in proposing their health, observed in impassioned accents: "What a country is this we live in! In other parts of the world there is no chance, except for men of high birth and aristocratic connections; but here, genius and industry are sure to be rewarded. See before you the examples of myself, the Chief Magistrate of the Metropolis of this great empire, and the Chief-Justice of England, sitting at my right hand,—both now in the highest offices of the state, and both sprung from the very dregs of the people!"

As a family man Lord Tenterden appears to great advantage: an attached husband and judicious father, he ever found his highest satisfaction and purest enjoy-

* Townsend *in loc.*

ments in his domestic circle. A pleasing evidence of this is given in the following verses, found among his papers, and probably written to his wife when he was on the circuit at Hereford:—

"In the noise of the bar, and the crowds of the hall,
Though destined still longer to move,
Let my thoughts wander home, and my memory recall
The dear pleasures of beauty and love.

The soft looks of my girl, the sweet voice of my boy,
Their antics, their hobbies, their sports;
How, the houses he builds, her quick fingers destroy,
And with kisses his pardon she courts.

With eyes full of tenderness, pleasure, and pride,
The fond mother sits watching their play;
Or turns, if I look not, my dulness to chide
And invites me, like them, to be gay.

She invites to be gay, and I yield to her voice,
And my toils and my sorrows forget:
In her beauty, her sweetness, her kindness rejoice,
And hallow the day that we met.

HEREFORD, *August* 6, 1800."

There is an anecdote related by Macready, the celebrated tragedian, which shows Lord Tenterden in a very amiable point of view. The narrator is describing a visit which he had paid to Canterbury Cathedral, under the escort of a verger, who, by reading and observation, had acquired a large amount of architectural and local knowledge; he thus proceeds:—"The guide directed my attention to everything worthy of notice; pointed out, with the detective eye of taste, the more recondite excellence of art throughout the building, and with convincing accuracy shed light on the historical traditions associated with it. It was opposite the western front that he stood with me before what seemed the site of a small shed or stall, then unoccupied, and said, 'Upon this spot a little barber's shop used to stand. The last time Lord Tenterden came down here he brought his son Charles with him, and it was my duty, of course, to attend them over the Cathedral.

"'When we came to this side of it, he led his son up to this very spot and said to him, "Charles, you see this little shop: I have brought you here on purpose to show it to you. In that shop your grandfather used to shave for a penny. That is the proudest reflection of my life. While you live never forget that, my dear Charles."'"

It is no small addition to the pleasing characteristics of this admirable man that he continued through life to preserve an ardent and unabated devotion to classical literature, "thus showing that the indulgence of such elegant tastes is consistent with a steady, and long continued, and successful application to abstruse juridical studies, and with the exemplary performance of the most laborious duties of an advocate and of a judge." In his busiest time Lord Tenterden would refresh himself in leisure hours by reading a satire of Juvenal, or a chorus of Euripides; he read poetry, especially the classics, with great feeling and taste, and wrote some elegant Latin poems on flowers and plants. In a letter to Sir E. Bridges, dated 15th September, 1830, he gave an interesting account of this "hobby":—

"I have always felt that it might be said that a Chief-Justice and a peer might employ his leisure hours better than in writing nonsense verses about flowers. But I must tell you how this fancy of recommencing to hammer Latin metres, after a cessation of more than thirty years, began. Brougham procured me from Lord Grenville a copy of some poems printed by him under the title of "Nugæ," chiefly his own, one or two, I believe, of Lord Wellesley's, written long ago, and a piece of very good Greek humour by Lord Holland. The motto in the title page is four or five hendœcasyllabic lines by Fabricius. At the same time, John Williams of the Northern Circuit, now the Queen's Solicitor-General, who is an admirable scholar, sent me four or five Greek epigrams of his own. I had a mind to thank each of them, and found I could do so with great ease to myself in ten hendœcasyllables. This led me to compose two trifles in the same metre on two favourite flowers, and afterwards some others, now I think twelve verses in all, in different Horatian metres, and one, an Ovidian epistle, of which the subject is the 'Forget me Not.' One of the earliest is an 'Ode on the Conservatory,' in the Alcaic metre, of which the last stanza contains the true cause and excuse of the whole, and this I will now transcribe,—

> 'Sit fabulosis fas mihi cantibus:
> Lenire curas! Sit mihi floribus
> Mulcere me fessum, senemque
> Carpere quos juvenis solebam.'"

Thus, to cheer his declining days, the aged Chief-Justice recurred to the pursuits of younger years and "dreamed he was a boy again."

To the end of his days his mental faculties remained wholly unimpaired, and he was determined "to die like a camel in the wilderness, with his burden on his back." An important Government prosecution connected with the Reform Bill riots at Bristol was appointed to be tried immediately before Michaelmas term, 1832. Notwithstanding his infirm health Lord Tenterden appeared on the bench with the other judges, and continued to preside during the first two days of the trial. On the third day he was seized with illness, and was put to bed, from which he never rose.

His disease baffled the skill of his medical attendants. He became delirious and talked very incoherently, and shortly before his death, his mind evidently reverting to the scene at which he had last assisted, he raised his head from his pillow, and in the slow and solemn tone in which he used to conclude his summing-up in cases of great importance, he said,—"And now, gentlemen of the jury, you will consider of your verdict."

These were his last words; when he had uttered them his head sank down, and in a few moments he expired without a groan. He had just entered upon his seventieth year at the time of his death.

Conclusion.

AMONG the remarkable doings of our great Lawyers we should not perhaps omit to notice the production of a valuable theological work by Sir Peter King, afterwards Lord Chancellor of England. This work is a learned and profound treatise upon the "Constitution and Discipline of the Primitive Church," in which the author endeavours to establish the usages of the early Christian assemblies within the first three centuries, by an appeal to the "authentic writings of those ages," and advocates the right of the Protestant Dissenters from episcopacy to be comprehended within the pale of the national establishment.

The work excited no small attention at the time of its appearance, passed through several editions, and called forth several learned answers. What is more—it has ever since continued to hold rank as the best treatise upon the subject, and not long ago I heard an erudite Non-con divine speaking in its praise, and saying that it has never been superseded.

There seems something strange at the present day in-the idea of a theological lawyer, and one is naturally disposed to inquire a little about the man and his history. Peter King was born in the year 1669 at Exeter, in which city his father Mr. Jerome King, carried on the business of a grocer and salter. He is said to have descended from a good family in Somersetshire; was a dissenter and a man of piety and worth, and was married to the sister of the illustrious John Locke. It was the intention of the good man to bring up his only son to his own business; and for some years the future Chancellor of Great Britain served in his father's shop. There are no authentic records of his early days, but it is reported that he quickly made a surprising proficiency in learning, being what is commonly called "a self-taught genius." We may be sure he searched his father's bookshelves, and probably found there a goodly number of books on divinity, to which study he early addicted himself, thus laying the foundation for his future distinction as the author of the "Inquiry into the Discipline of the Primitive Church."

As he advanced towards manhood he was noticed with friendly regard by his celebrated kinsman, who, finding in the lad abilities of no common order, advised that he should be sent to the University of Leyden, where he continued some years in the diligent pursuit of his studies. After the lapse of more than a century and a half it is difficult to trace with accuracy those minute features of character which bring us, so to speak, personally acquainted with the individual man. Of Lord Chancellor King few such traits are preserved. That he was admirable in his domestic relationships, we gather from the ardent affection with which he inspired his great relative, who addressed to him a number of letters directing and counselling him in every important step of his life, and finally wrote to him, shortly before his own decease, the following touching epistle.

"*June* 1, 1704.

". . . . . I remember it is the end of a term, a busy time with you, and you intend to be here speedily, which is better than writing at a distance. Pray be sure to order your matters so as to spend all the next week with me; as far as I can impartially guess, it will be the last week I am ever like to have with you; for, if I mistake not, I have very little time left in the world. This comfortable, and to me usually restorative, season of the year has no effect upon me for the better: on the contrary, all appearances concur to warn me that the dissolution of this cottage is not far off. Refuse not, therefore, to help me to pass some of the last hours of my life as easily as may be, in the conversation of one who is not only the nearest, but the dearest to me of any man in the world. I have a great many things to talk with you about, which I can talk to nobody else about. I therefore desire you again, deny not this to my affection. I know nothing at such a time so desirable and so useful as the conversation of a friend one loves and relies on."

Such confidence and attachment on the part of the dying philosopher, testify in an unmistakeable manner the worth and true excellence of King. At the time of Locke's decease he had reached his 35th year, and was just settled in a happy marriage. He had already attained to great eminence at the bar, and was the acknowledged leader of the Western Circuit, and a short time after was elected Recorder of London, and knighted by Queen Anne. In the year 1714 he was raised to the dignity of Lord Chief-Justice of Common Pleas, which he enjoyed for a period of eleven years, and acquitted himself in his high office to the universal satisfaction, being acknowledged on all hands to merit the highest praise as a common law judge. We are assured that his judgments, as handed down in the reports, are "marked by great precision of definition, subtlety of distinction, breadth of principle, lucidness of arrangement and felicity of illustration."

On the impeachment and conviction of Lord Macclesfield, who had held the Great Seal, Sir Peter King was made Lord Chancellor, and a peer; but he did not in his new capacity satisfy public expectation; and is said to have injured his health by his laborious efforts to master the especial department of professional learning, necessary for the performance of his new duties. His death happened in the sixty-sixth year of his age, shortly after he had resigned the cares of office in consequence of a paralytic seizure which gave warning that his end was approaching.

He rose from obscurity to distinction and honours, solely by his own energy and worth; and he was beloved for his goodness and amiability. An example worthy of the imitation of any youthful spirit which aspires to surmount the obstacles of poverty and humble birth, and to attain a place among the good and the prosperous. He himself ascribed all his success in life to his laborious endeavours, and he took for his motto the very characteristic and fitting one; " Labor ipse voluptas," which gave occasion to the following lines :—

" 'Tis not the splendour of the place,
The gilded coach, the purse, the mace,
Nor all the pompous train of state
With crowds that at your levee wait,
That make you happy, make you great.
But whilst mankind you strive to bless
With all the talent you possess;
Whilst the chief joy that you receive
Arises from the joy you give;
This takes the heart, and conquering spite,
Makes e'en the heavy burden light;
For pleasure—rightly understood—
Is only Labour to do Good."

THE END